The House of Representatives

KNOW YOUR GOVERNMENT

The House of Representatives

Bruce A. Ragsdale

CHELSEA HOUSE PUBLISHERS

Chelsea House Publishers
Editor-in-Chief: Nancy Toff
Executive Editor: Remmel T. Nunn
Managing Editor: Karyn Gullen Browne
Copy Chief: Juliann Barbato
Picture Editor: Adrian G. Allen
Art Director: Maria Epes
Manufacturing Manager: Gerald Levine

Know Your Government
Senior Editor: Kathy Kuhtz

Staff for THE HOUSE OF REPRESENTATIVES
Associate Editor: Pierre Hauser
Copy Editor: Karen Hammonds
Deputy Copy Chief: Ellen Scordato
Editorial Assistant: Theodore Keyes
Picture Researcher: Anne Hobart
Assistant Art Director: Laurie Jewell
Designer: Noreen M. Lamb
Layout: Donna Sinisgalli
Production Coordinator: Joseph Romano

3 5 7 9 8 6 4 2

Library of Congress Cataloging in Publication Data

Ragsdale, Bruce A.
  The House of Representatives.

  (Know your government)
  Bibliography: p.
  Includes index.
  Summary: Surveys the history of the House of Representatives and describes its structure, current function, and influence on American society.
    1. United States. Congress. House—Juvenile literature. [1. United States. Congress. House] I. Title. II. Series: Know your government (New York, N.Y.)
JK1319.R33 1989   328.73′072   87-24976
ISBN 1-55546-112-3
     0-7910-0866-5 (pbk.)

CONTENTS

KNOW YOUR GOVERNMENT

CHELSEA HOUSE PUBLISHERS

INTRODUCTION

Government: Crises of Confidence

Arthur M. Schlesinger, jr.

From the start, Americans have regarded their government with a mixture of reliance and mistrust. The men who founded the republic did not doubt the indispensability of government. "If men were angels," observed the 51st Federalist Paper, "no government would be necessary." But men are not angels. Because human beings are subject to wicked as well as to noble impulses, government was deemed essential to assure freedom and order.

At the same time, the American revolutionaries knew that government could also become a source of injury and oppression. The men who gathered in Philadelphia in 1787 to write the Constitution therefore had two purposes in mind. They wanted to establish a strong central authority and to limit that central authority's capacity to abuse its power.

To prevent the abuse of power, the Founding Fathers wrote two basic principles into the new Constitution. The principle of federalism divided power between the state governments and the central authority. The principle of the separation of powers subdivided the central authority itself into three branches—the executive, the legislative, and the judiciary—so that "each may be a check on the other." The *Know Your Government* series focuses on the major executive departments and agencies in these branches of the federal government.

The Constitution did not plan the executive branch in any detail. After vesting the executive power in the president, it assumed the existence of "executive departments" without specifying what these departments should be. Congress began defining their functions in 1789 by creating the Departments of State, Treasury, and War. The secretaries in charge of these departments made up President Washington's first cabinet. Congress also provided for a legal officer, and President Washington soon invited the attorney general, as he was called, to attend cabinet meetings. As need required, Congress created more executive departments.

Setting up the cabinet was only the first step in organizing the American state. With almost no guidance from the Constitution, President Washington, seconded by Alexander Hamilton, his brilliant secretary of the treasury, equipped the infant republic with a working administrative structure. The Federalists believed in both executive energy and executive accountability and set high standards for public appointments. The Jeffersonian opposition had less faith in strong government and preferred local government to the central authority. But when Jefferson himself became president in 1801, although he set out to change the direction of policy, he found no reason to alter the framework the Federalists had erected.

By 1801 there were about 3,000 federal civilian employees in a nation of a little more than 5 million people. Growth in territory and population steadily enlarged national responsibilities. Thirty years later, when Jackson was president, there were more than 11,000 government workers in a nation of 13 million. The federal establishment was increasing at a faster rate than the population.

Jackson's presidency brought significant changes in the federal service. He believed that the executive branch contained too many officials who saw their jobs as "species of property" and as "a means of promoting individual interest." Against the idea of a permanent service based on life tenure, Jackson argued for the periodic redistribution of federal offices, contending that this was the democratic way and that official duties could be made "so plain and simple that men of intelligence may readily qualify themselves for their performance." He called this policy rotation-in-office. His opponents called it the spoils system.

In fact, partisan legend exaggerated the extent of Jackson's removals. More than 80 percent of federal officeholders retained their jobs. Jackson discharged no larger a proportion of government workers than Jefferson had done a generation earlier. But the rise in these years of mass political parties gave federal patronage new importance as a means of building the party and of rewarding activists. Jackson's successors were less restrained in the distribu-

8

tion of spoils. As the federal establishment grew—to nearly 40,000 by 1861—the politicization of the public service excited increasing concern.

After the Civil War the spoils system became a major political issue. High-minded men condemned it as the root of all political evil. The spoilsmen, said the British commentator James Bryce, "have distorted and depraved the mechanism of politics." Patronage, by giving jobs to unqualified, incompetent, and dishonest persons, lowered the standards of public service and nourished corrupt political machines. Office-seekers pursued presidents and cabinet secretaries without mercy. "Patronage," said Ulysses S. Grant after his presidency, "is the bane of the presidential office." "Every time I appoint someone to office," said another political leader, "I make a hundred enemies and one ingrate." George William Curtis, the president of the National Civil Service Reform League, summed up the indictment. He said,

> The theory which perverts public trusts into party spoils, making public employment dependent upon personal favor and not on proved merit, necessarily ruins the self-respect of public employees, destroys the function of party in a republic, prostitutes elections into a desperate strife for personal profit, and degrades the national character by lowering the moral tone and standard of the country.

The object of civil service reform was to promote efficiency and honesty in the public service and to bring about the ethical regeneration of public life. Over bitter opposition from politicians, the reformers in 1883 passed the Pendleton Act, establishing a bipartisan Civil Service Commission, competitive examinations, and appointment on merit. The Pendleton Act also gave the president authority to extend by executive order the number of "classified" jobs—that is, jobs subject to the merit system. The act applied initially only to about 14,000 of the more than 100,000 federal positions. But by the end of the 19th century 40 percent of federal jobs had moved into the classified category.

Civil service reform was in part a response to the growing complexity of American life. As society grew more organized and problems more technical, official duties were no longer so plain and simple that any person of intelligence could perform them. In public service, as in other areas, the all-round man was yielding ground to the expert, the amateur to the professional. The excesses of the spoils system thus provoked the counter-ideal of scientific public administration, separate from politics and, as far as possible, insulated against it.

The cult of the expert, however, had its own excesses. The idea that administration could be divorced from policy was an illusion. And in the realm of policy, the expert, however much segregated from partisan politics, can

9

never attain perfect objectivity. He remains the prisoner of his own set of values. It is these values rather than technical expertise that determine fundamental judgments of public policy. To turn over such judgments to experts, moreover, would be to abandon democracy itself; for in a democracy final decisions must be made by the people and their elected representatives. "The business of the expert," the British political scientist Harold Laski rightly said, "is to be on tap and not on top."

Politics, however, were deeply ingrained in American folkways. This meant intermittent tension between the presidential government, elected every four years by the people, and the permanent government, which saw presidents come and go while it went on forever. Sometimes the permanent government knew better than its political masters; sometimes it opposed or sabotaged valuable new initiatives. In the end a strong president with effective cabinet secretaries could make the permanent government responsive to presidential purpose, but it was often an exasperating struggle.

The struggle within the executive branch was less important, however, than the growing impatience with bureaucracy in society as a whole. The 20th century saw a considerable expansion of the federal establishment. The Great Depression and the New Deal led the national government to take on a variety of new responsibilities. The New Deal extended the federal regulatory apparatus. By 1940, in a nation of 130 million people, the number of federal workers for the first time passed the 1 million mark. The Second World War brought federal civilian employment to 3.8 million in 1945. With peace, the federal establishment declined to around 2 million by 1950. Then growth resumed, reaching 2.8 million by the 1980s.

The New Deal years saw rising criticism of "big government" and "bureaucracy." Businessmen resented federal regulation. Conservatives worried about the impact of paternalistic government on individual self-reliance, on community responsibility, and on economic and personal freedom. The nation in effect renewed the old debate between Hamilton and Jefferson in the early republic, although with an ironic exchange of positions. For the Hamiltonian constituency, the "rich and well-born," once the advocate of affirmative government, now condemned government intervention, while the Jeffersonian constituency, the plain people, once the advocate of a weak central government and of states' rights, now favored government intervention.

In the 1980s, with the presidency of Ronald Reagan, the debate has burst out with unusual intensity. According to conservatives, government intervention abridges liberty, stifles enterprise, and is inefficient, wasteful, and arbitrary. It disturbs the harmony of the self-adjusting market and creates worse troubles than it solves. Get government off our backs, according to the popular cliché, and our problems will solve themselves. When government is necessary, let it be at the local level, close to the people. Above all, stop the inexorable growth of the federal government.

In fact, for all the talk about the "swollen" and "bloated" bureaucracy, the federal establishment has not been growing as inexorably as many Americans seem to believe. In 1949, it consisted of 2.1 million people. Thirty years later, while the country had grown by 70 million, the federal force had grown only by 750,000. Federal workers were a smaller percentage of the population in 1985 than they were in 1955—or in 1940. The federal establishment, in short, has not kept pace with population growth. Moreover, national defense and the postal service account for 60 percent of federal employment.

Why then the widespread idea about the remorseless growth of government? It is partly because in the 1960s the national government assumed new and intrusive functions: affirmative action in civil rights, environmental protection, safety and health in the workplace, community organization, legal aid to the poor. Although this enlargement of the federal regulatory role was accompanied by marked growth in the size of government on all levels, the expansion has taken place primarily in state and local government. Whereas the federal force increased by only 27 percent in the 30 years after 1950, the state and local government force increased by an astonishing 212 percent.

Despite the statistics, the conviction flourishes in some minds that the national government is a steadily growing behemoth swallowing up the liberties of the people. The foes of Washington prefer local government, feeling it is closer to the people and therefore allegedly more responsive to popular needs. Obviously there is a great deal to be said for settling local questions locally. But local government is characteristically the government of the locally powerful. Historically, the way the locally powerless have won their human and constitutional rights has often been through appeal to the national government. The national government has vindicated racial justice against local bigotry, defended the Bill of Rights against local vigilantism, and protected natural resources against local greed. It has civilized industry and secured the rights of labor organizations. Had the states' rights creed prevailed, there would perhaps still be slavery in the United States.

The national authority, far from diminishing the individual, has given most Americans more personal dignity and liberty than ever before. The individual freedoms destroyed by the increase in national authority have been in the main

11

the freedom to deny black Americans their rights as citizens; the freedom to put small children to work in mills and immigrants in sweatshops; the freedom to pay starvation wages, require barbarous working hours, and permit squalid working conditions; the freedom to deceive in the sale of goods and securities; the freedom to pollute the environment—all freedoms that, one supposes, a civilized nation can readily do without.

"Statements are made," said President John F. Kennedy in 1963, "labelling the Federal Government an outsider, an intruder, an adversary. . . . The United States Government is not a stranger or not an enemy. It is the people of fifty states joining in a national effort. . . . Only a great national effort by a great people working together can explore the mysteries of space, harvest the products at the bottom of the ocean, and mobilize the human, natural, and material resources of our lands."

So an old debate continues. However, Americans are of two minds. When pollsters ask large, spacious questions—Do you think government has become too involved in your lives? Do you think government should stop regulating business?—a sizable majority opposes big government. But when asked specific questions about the practical work of government—Do you favor social security? unemployment compensation? Medicare? health and safety standards in factories? environmental protection? government guarantee of jobs for everyone seeking employment? price and wage controls when inflation threatens?—a sizable majority approves of intervention.

In general, Americans do not want less government. What they want is more efficient government. They want government to do a better job. For a time in the 1970s, with Vietnam and Watergate, Americans lost confidence in the national government. In 1964, more than three-quarters of those polled had thought the national government could be trusted to do right most of the time. By 1980 only one-quarter was prepared to offer such trust. But by 1984 trust in the federal government to manage national affairs had climbed back to 45 percent.

Bureaucracy is a term of abuse. But it is impossible to run any large organization, whether public or private, without a bureaucracy's division of labor and hierarchy of authority. And we live in a world of large organizations. Without bureaucracy modern society would collapse. The problem is not to abolish bureaucracy, but to make it flexible, efficient, and capable of innovation.

Two hundred years after the drafting of the Constitution, Americans still regard government with a mixture of reliance and mistrust—a good combination. Mistrust is the best way to keep government reliable. Informed criticism is the means of correcting governmental inefficiency, incompetence, and arbitrariness; that is, of best enabling government to play its essential role. For without government, we cannot attain the goals of the Founding Fathers. Without an understanding of government, we cannot have the informed criticism that makes government do the job right. It is the duty of every American citizen to know our government—which is what this series is all about.

Vice-president George Bush (left) and Speaker of the House James Wright listen to President Ronald Reagan's State of the Union message on December 27, 1987.

ONE

"The First Branch of the Legislature"

Today, the House of Representatives is the branch of government most closely tied to the people, with 435 voting members drawn from the 50 states. The framers of the Constitution established the House of Representatives and the Senate as the two houses of the legislature in 1789. They deliberately separated the powers of the government among three independent branches—the legislative, the executive, and the judicial—because they believed it was necessary to prevent any one branch from assuming too much power and authority. The framers called the House of Representatives the "first branch of the legislature" because it provided for the participation of the people and would be held accountable to them. The popular election of the members of the House every two years continues to provide the most direct form of representative democracy. This concept of representation, by which the voters select a delegate to represent their interests in the proceedings of the government, allows the people to control the arm of government responsible for making laws.

When the Senate first convened in 1789, its members were chosen by state legislatures—two senators from each state—and met in secret. Senators represented states rather than individuals and were intended to deliberate over legislation more carefully than would be possible in the House of Representa-

The United States Congress met for the first time in New York in 1789, two years after the framers of the Constitution created the two houses of the legislature—the House of Representatives and the Senate.

tives, the larger and often more boisterous branch. In 1913, however, the Seventeenth Amendment to the Constitution altered this process and senators were elected by the people. Today, there are 100 senators, and sessions are televised, giving the American public a closer view of the legislative procedures of the Senate.

In contrast, the House of Representatives is the only elected branch of government that gives every voter an equal voice—each member of the House represents the same number of constituents (residents in a representative's district). Through the allocation of legislative seats, or apportionment, representatives are distributed among the states according to population. Under the Apportionment Act of 1929, Congress fixed the number of House seats at 435 and established the redistribution of the seats among the 50 states by the Census Bureau after each decennial (every 10 years) census. After the reapportionment decisions have been made, each state that gains or loses seats in the House must be redistricted by its state legislature. The under- or overrepresentation of states in the House is thus avoided through the reapportionment by the Bureau of the Census.

The historical development of the House of Representatives reinforced its popular character. Frequently throughout American history the House has served as the central forum for discussion of the most important issues of the day. In the first 50 years of the federal government, the House forged the way in establishing a strong national union. In later years it continued to respond to popular demands for reform and new governmental programs. As the source of all federal laws, Congress influences the lives of all Americans. The House of Representatives has a special significance because of its authority to initiate all legislation concerning federal taxes and government spending. The framers of the Constitution granted the House power over matters of money because the two-year term of this half of Congress keeps every member in constant contact with the voters. It was the issue of taxation without representation that had thrust the American colonists into the War of Independence.

During the mid-18th century, England tried to tighten colonial administration and to raise money by levying duties on numerous imports into the colonies. The colonists bitterly opposed these intrusions, particularly because they were not given the right to elect members to represent them in Parliament. According to the theory of government that some colonists at that time believed, King George III and Parliament had broken their pact with the American colonies because they no longer protected the people's rights of "life, liberty, and the pursuit of happiness." By breaking this pact, the king had freed the colonists from their allegiance to him.

The American colonists often quoted the writings of John Locke, an English philosopher who wrote during the time of England's Glorious Revolution (1688–89), in defense of their own rights. Locke, in his *Two Treatises on Government* (1690), discredited the divine right of kings—the theory of government whereby the king receives the right to rule directly from God and not from the people. Locke believed that the consent of the people is the only true basis of any government's right to rule, and if the government betrays the people's trust then it is the people's duty to rebel and overthrow it in order to preserve their rights. Locke's view had a profound effect on the American colonists and is reflected in the Declaration of Independence. Written by Thomas Jefferson and adopted July 4, 1776, this document proclaimed the birth of a new nation, one that would derive its "powers from the consent of the governed."

Today, the vote for representatives continues to be the most frequent opportunity for voters to express their opinions on the federal level. The apportionment of House seats based on population allows this body to reflect the changing distribution of population in the United States. The large number of representatives, frequent elections, and shifting of seats from one state to another do not contribute to the efficiency of the legislature, but they do allow a broad and representative range of opinions to be heard within the national government.

To study the evolution of the House of Representatives is to traverse the course of American history, from its birth at the Constitutional Convention to its transformation into a modern and complex institution that continues to carry out the constitutional mandate of representative democracy.

A French minister meets members of the Continental Congress in 1778. Until the U.S. Constitution was ratified by the states in 1788, this unicameral body was the nation's sole legislature.

TWO

The Constitutional Convention and the House of Representatives

The delegates to the Constitutional Convention in Philadelphia during the summer of 1787 designed the House of Representatives to be the popular foundation for the new federal government. The delegates agreed that the new government should be a representative democracy or, as they called it, a republic. A popularly elected house in Congress would guarantee the people a regular voice in the government and ensure that the final power in the national government would always be in the hands of the voting population, through a series of checks that the House held over those branches of government not subject to popular election, such as the presidency and, until 1913, the Senate. (The president of the United States is chosen by the electoral votes of states. In the electoral college, where each state has a vote equal to the number of its senators and representatives, small states have a disproportionate voice.)

However, the delegates of the Constitutional Convention were acutely aware that they did not want the "masses," or a majority faction, to take control of the new government. Such a faction would need to win control, in a series of elections, of the Senate, presidency, and perhaps the Supreme Court in order to become tyrannical. The delegates believed that the separation of powers, or that assigning constitutional authority to the legislative, executive, and judicial branches, was not enough to prevent officials with different powers of authority from acting together in a despotic way. To solve their dilemma, the delegates devised the system of checks and balances whereby each branch of the government was given some role in the operations of the others. For example, Congress enacts laws, but the president has the power to veto them. The Supreme Court is able to declare laws passed by Congress and approved by the president to be unconstitutional, but the president appoints the justices of the Supreme Court with the Senate's consent. The president executes the laws, but Congress appropriates the money. Furthermore, the House and the Senate have the power to veto each other in the enactment of a law, but a bill must be passed by both houses before it can be given to the president for his signature.

The earliest settlers in the British colonies brought with them an English faith in the legislature as the best protection of a people's liberty. In America, the legislatures, or assemblies, of each colony took on an added importance because the lower house of each assembly was the only branch of government controlled by the residents of the colony. By the mid-18th century, the popularly elected houses of the colonial assemblies were the most important defense against royal authority. Americans used their colonial legislatures, with their power to raise and spend money, as a means to check royal governors and limit imperial control.

In England, Parliament is divided into the House of Commons, whose members are elected by the people, and the House of Lords, whose members are hereditary peers, or nobles. During the 18th century, members of the House of Commons (also known as the lower house) frequently did not live in their election districts and were thought by the king to represent only the general good of all countrymen. In America, colonial legislatures expanded to include representatives from newly settled areas, and members of the assembly were often required to reside in their election districts. Voters in America came to expect the legislators to represent the interests of particular communities.

After independence, when the Americans established new governments on the state level and created the first national government, they gave the state legislatures more power than the national government. In the hope of

20

An exterior view of the houses of Parliament in London, England. American colonists incorporated many aspects of the British parliamentary system into the Articles of Confederation, ratified by the states in 1781.

preventing the abuse of executive authority seen under British rule, the first national government did not even provide for an executive branch or a judicial branch. Under the Articles of Confederation, which was the charter for the national government from 1781 to 1789, the Continental Congress, in which each state had a single vote, was the sole legislative body granted authority over the states and in dealings with foreign nations. However, the Articles of Confederation attempted to preserve the authority of the states, and Congress was given only those powers that the states were willing to relinquish: all powers connected with war and peace and the power to establish post offices and charge postage, to set standards of weights and measures, and to coin money. Nevertheless, Congress was not given the authority to collect taxes to support a war.

The placement of all governmental jurisdiction, or authority, in one legislature and the failure of the Articles of Confederation to grant Congress power to raise revenue or regulate commerce among the states were the principal reasons for calling a Constitutional Convention to consider a new form of national government. Yet when the 55 delegates met in the summer of 1787 they fully agreed that the legislature should continue to be the basis of a republican form of government. The proper structure of Congress was the subject of the first major debate at the convention, and the first article of the Constitution established the House of Representatives and the Senate.

The great majority of delegates agreed that the new Congress should consist of two houses rather than the unicameral (single house) legislature in existence under the Articles of Confederation. Most states had followed the English model in establishing bicameral, or two-house, legislatures. The exact distinctions

James Madison, one of Virginia's delegates to the Constitutional Convention in 1787. At the convention, Madison proposed that one branch of the legislature consist of popularly elected representatives; the number of seats allotted to each state would be in proportion to its population.

between the House and Senate were the subject of extensive debate, but the delegates agreed the House of Representatives would be the "first branch" of the legislature. In England and the American colonies, the popular half of the legislature was known as the lower house because it represented the common people rather than the aristocracy, whose province was the upper house. The delegates at the Constitutional Convention rejected all references to upper and lower houses and spoke only of a first and second branch to refer to the House and Senate, respectively. James Madison, James Wilson, and the other men who were determined to establish a national government superior to the states dominated the convention. They considered the House the first branch because it embodied the democratic participation that defined a republic. Throughout the debate on the structure of the House of Representatives, the delegates expressed their belief that the power and organization of the popularly elected branch would largely define the role of the new national government.

At the convention, debate on the House of Representatives centered on key questions regarding the proper basis of representation and the manner and frequency of election to the legislature. Madison's proposal, embodied in the Virginia Plan submitted to the convention by the chairman of the Virginia delegation, Edmund Randolph, suggested a House of Representatives apportioned on the basis of population and popularly elected every three years. The provision for representation on the basis of population provoked the most serious debate during the convention. Delegates from small states feared proportional representation would give the most populous states control over the new government. William Paterson, a delegate from New Jersey, offered a counterproposal that would have granted each state equal representation in a unicameral legislature, like that under the Articles of Confederation.

Those delegates who wished to create a stronger national government understood that more was at stake than a conflict of interests between large and small states. Only proportional representation based on population would create a national basis for the government, as opposed to a state-based confederation, as well as help the federal Congress gain the popular allegiance necessary to successfully carry out its expanded powers. Madison, Wilson, and others hoped proportional representation in both houses of Congress would limit the authority of all states, large or small, to local affairs.

One point of dispute over representation sprang from sectional conflict, which was far more serious than that between large and small states. Southerners insisted that slaves be counted among a state's population when seats were apportioned in the House of Representatives. Most northern delegates believed the importation of slaves should end, but they agreed to a

Chained slaves walk down a street in Washington, D.C., in the 1800s. Constitutional Convention delegates agreed to allow southern states to count three-fifths of their slave populations in determining House apportionment, but only if the same number of slaves were used to calculate the taxes the states would pay to the national government.

compromise that allowed slave states to include three-fifths of the slave population in the formula for representation. In return, southerners accepted a provision that would include the same three-fifths of the slave population in determining direct taxation.

The convention delegates reached a final agreement on representation in Congress through the so-called Great Compromise developed by a committee of the convention. In the compromise, which was accepted on July 16, 1787, the delegates agreed to Madison's proposal for proportional representation in the House of Representatives and Connecticut delegate Roger Sherman's suggestion that each state have equal representation in the Senate—one senator per state. The provisions for Senate representation prevented Madison from creating a national legislature that disregarded the states, but the creation of the House of Representatives was a victory for him and the other nationalists.

The delegates again divided over the issue of elections to the House of Representatives. Madison, Wilson, and Alexander Hamilton of New York insisted that one branch of the new government be popularly elected in order to establish a truly republican form of government and secure popular

Constitutional Convention delegate Elbridge Gerry of Massachusetts opposed Madison's suggestion for a House elected by the people. Gerry had little faith in the public's ability to elect competent government officials.

allegiance to the central government. George Mason of Virginia said that the House should be the "grand depository of the democratic principle of the Government."

Elbridge Gerry of Massachusetts and Roger Sherman did not believe the people had the wisdom to select national leaders. These men led the faction that favored election of House members by the state legislatures, as members in the Continental Congress had been.

Hamilton was convinced the opposition to popular election was an attempt to limit the national government's authority over the states. Madison agreed that direct election of one house in the legislature was necessary to establish the federal government's control over the states. The arguments in favor of federal supremacy and the growth of democratic participation following independence persuaded a majority of the delegates to approve popular election of House members. In the Senate, which was designed to preserve a measure of state sovereignty, members were to be elected by the state legislatures.

Madison was not successful, however, in persuading the convention delegates to approve his proposal for a three-year term for House members. During their struggles against the British Parliament (in which members of the House of Commons held their seats for four or more years without standing for reelection), Americans became convinced that annual elections were the best means of preventing an abuse of power by the legislature. Madison believed the Constitution would provide sufficient checks on the House of Representatives to permit a longer term. He also wanted to give members time to meet their responsibilities in both the capital and their home districts. The convention delegates thought three years was too long an interval between elections but agreed to the desirability of longer terms in a large republic. The final Constitution provided for House elections every two years. This frequency of election became a critical factor in the development of the House and remains a distinguishing characteristic of this branch of the legislature. Every two years the House becomes a new legislature whereas the Senate is a continuing body with internal rules and procedures applying to successive Congresses.

On September 17, 1787, the delegates signed a final draft of the Constitution that granted the House of Representatives the powers necessary to unite the people under a strong national government. The qualifications for office and for voting made the House the most democratic and accessible branch of the new government. The Constitution allowed states to define voting requirements but ordered that they be no more restrictive than those established for participation in the election of the larger branch of the state legislature. Many states required property ownership to qualify for voting, but the convention

26

Convention delegates sign the U.S. Constitution on September 17, 1787. The national charter set forth guidelines for a strong federal government consisting of three separate branches: the executive, legislative, and judicial.

delegates refused to include this restriction in the Constitution, thus opening the way for universal suffrage, or at least voting privileges for all adult, white males.

According to the Constitution, members of the House needed to be at least 25 years of age—5 years younger than the minimum age set for senators. Members were required to be American citizens for seven years before election and residents of the state they represented. The convention delegates rejected proposals to require members to be property owners.

As the most democratic branch of the government, the House of Representatives received special powers and privileges under the Constitution. The most important privilege of the House has been its exclusive power to originate all bills to raise revenue. The nationalists at the Constitutional Convention insisted the House receive this authority in return for the equal representation of states in the Senate. At one point in the convention the delegates decided to give the House sole power to originate bills appropriating, or distributing, government funds as well. In the final draft of the Constitution the framers omitted this clause, but in practice the House has assumed the right to initiate spending bills. The House was also granted sole power to impeach (formally charge with misconduct in office) the president or other officers of the government. Once the House votes articles of impeachment against an official, the Senate conducts a trial to determine guilt or innocence and can convict an impeached official upon a two-thirds majority vote. Under the Constitution, the House of Representatives enjoys full control over its own rules and procedures. Unlike the Senate, which is presided over by the vice-president, the House elects its own presiding officer, the Speaker of the House. The representatives have sole power to censure or expel one of their fellow members, regardless of popular opinion.

The House of Representatives shared with the Senate a number of sweeping powers intended to overcome the weaknesses that plagued the congress of the Articles of Confederation. The Constitution granted Congress authority to regulate the commerce of the United States with foreign nations. Congress was also allowed to borrow money and to pay off the national debt, which had become a symbol of the ineffective government run under the Articles of Confederation. Congress could further enhance the credibility of the federal government by coining money and regulating the value of such currency. The two houses of Congress held the sole power to declare war and to raise and support armies. In an important provision designed to encourage national expansion, Congress received the power to admit new states as equal members of the Union, rather than dependent territories. These powers ensured that the national legislature would be able to secure the government's authority over the states.

Following independence from Great Britain, the sweeping powers granted legislatures under the state constitutions had taught Americans that even a democratically elected legislature would abuse power if it were unchecked. In order to prevent tyranny on the part of the legislature at the federal level, the Constitution limited the authority of the House of Representatives but at the same time granted it power denied the Continental Congress. Unlike the Continental Congress, the federal Congress was checked by the president's ability to veto legislation unless two-thirds of both houses of Congress voted to override the veto. An independent judiciary, described in Article III of the Constitution and established by the Judiciary Act of 1789, could also render decisions against Congress. In response to the special concerns of a generation that had opposed British power, the Constitution included specific restrictions on the powers of the House and Senate. The Constitution forbade Congress from suspending the writ of habeas corpus (a protection against arrest without formal charges), except in time of war and then only for one year. Congress was also unable to issue a bill of attainder which was a means of convicting individuals of a crime without a trial. (In other words, Congress could not exercise a judicial function of determining guilt and pronouncing a sentence.) Like the Continental Congress, the federal Congress was forbidden to grant any titles of nobility. Although the House of Representatives received broad powers to raise and appropriate money, the Constitution demanded that all appropriations be made through law, and the House was required to regularly account for all of its financial proceedings.

After the states ratified the Constitution in 1788, the Continental Congress set the date for the inauguration of the federal government, March 4, 1789, and the individual states established procedures for the first election of House members. In some states, representatives were chosen from districts, and in others the candidates ran on statewide, or at-large, tickets. Whatever the arrangements, the first House elections provided for the only direct, popular participation in the new government at a time when all senators and most presidential electors were chosen by the state legislatures. The biennial (every two years) election of House members quickly encouraged involvement in the federal government and fulfilled the founders' hope for a broad base upon which the federal system might rest.

Frederick A. C. Muhlenberg was elected the first Speaker of the House in 1789. Delegates expected the Speaker to look after House business and administer the rules of debate.

THREE

The House of Representatives and the Growth of the Nation

The members of the House of Representatives who arrived in the first national capital, New York City, for the opening of the First Congress on March 4, 1789, faced the task of translating the written Constitution into a working system of government. The representatives and senators elected to the first House were responsible for putting the rest of the government into operation. These men had wide legislative experience on both the state and national levels. Of the 65 members who eventually took their seats in the House, 36 had served in the Continental Congress, and 9 had been delegates to the convention that drew up the new Constitution. Thirty-nine members of the first House had served in the legislature of their state. The First Congress was fortunate to have men of great dedication who would contribute to the success of the new government. No member was more important than James Madison (representative from Virginia, 1789–97), who had already played the leading role in drafting the Constitution and now would take charge of setting in motion the new government.

On April 1, 1789, a majority of the House members had reached New York City and thus constituted a quorum (the minimum number of members necessary to legislate). The first job was to elect a Speaker of the House to preside over the business of the house and enforce the rules of debate. The members in attendance chose as their first Speaker Frederick A. C. Muhlenberg, a Lutheran minister from Pennsylvania who had been president of the state convention that ratified the Constitution on behalf of Pennsylvania. The House members elected other officers, agreed to their first rules of debate, and quickly moved on to consider legislation to establish the authority of the new government.

Following the procedure set out in the Constitution, the House of Representatives and the Senate counted the electoral votes for the first president and arranged for the inauguration of George Washington (1732–99) on April 30, 1789. Even after Washington's inauguration, Congress played an important role in forming the executive branch of government. During the spring and summer of 1789, Congress created the cabinet departments of State, Treasury, and War, the secretaries of which were then appointed by President Washington. Again, James Madison was the most important figure in defining the legislation establishing these executive departments, especially the Treasury Department, which was granted the kind of power (for example, raising and managing revenue) denied to the government under the Articles of Confederation. The House of Representatives and the Senate were also responsible for the creation of a third branch of government: The Constitution called for a Supreme Court and a system of lower federal courts to be established by Congress. In the Judiciary Act of 1789 Congress provided for a Supreme Court of six members and a system of circuit and district courts that would hear federal cases on a regional basis. (A circuit court is a state's general trial court that serves several counties—its judges go on "circuit," or travel, from one county to another.)

In addition to setting up the government departments specified in the Constitution, the First Congress made an important addition to the Constitution itself. During the debates over the contents of the Constitution, many Americans approved the new system of government on the condition that it contain a bill of rights. In the summer of 1789, Madison presented the House of Representatives with a series of constitutional amendments designed to protect basic liberties of individuals and the states. After approval by the House and Senate, Madison's amendments were submitted to the states for ratification as part of the Constitution. By December 1791, three-quarters of the states had ratified the 10 amendments now known as the Bill of Rights.

The Bill of Rights, consisting of the first ten amendments to the Constitution, was ratified by the states in 1791. These declarations of rights—for example, the freedoms of religion and speech—are shared by all citizens and cannot be violated by the government.

After organizing the structure of the new government, the House of Representatives approved a variety of legislation designed to make the United States a strong national power. The House's first significant action was to establish duties, or taxes, on trade in order to regulate commerce with foreign nations and bring in revenue. The lack of authority over economic affairs was the greatest source of weakness in the Articles of Confederation, and Madison and Secretary of the Treasury Alexander Hamilton were determined to give the new government control over fiscal, or financial, policy. Following a series

Federal Hall in New York City. The First Congress met here on March 4, 1789, but then voted to move the nation's capital temporarily to Philadelphia.

of reports by Hamilton, the House and Senate provided for the payment of the national debt and founded the Bank of the United States to encourage commercial development and manufacturing in the young nation. Among the other accomplishments of this remarkably productive Congress were the creation of a regular census and the admission of Kentucky and Vermont to statehood. Great public interest centered on the First Congress's search for a permanent capital. Despite New York City's efforts to keep the seat of government there, Congress voted to move the capital to Philadelphia for 10 years while a new federal city was built on the banks of the Potomac River in Maryland. On December 6, 1790, the third session of the First Congress convened in chambers next to Independence Hall in Philadelphia. The House continued to meet in what became known as Congress Hall until November

1800, when the Sixth Congress met in the unfinished Capitol building in Washington, D.C.

As these early Congresses addressed the wide-ranging problems before the federal government, members of the House of Representatives recognized that the larger of the two houses of Congress needed a strong internal organization in order to operate effectively. Membership increased from 65 to 106 in 1792 and to 142 after the census of 1800. If the diverse interests present in such a large body were to produce legislation, it was necessary to find the means to draw agreement from a majority of the congressmen. From the First Congress to the present day, the history of the House of Representatives has been the story of attempts to balance the expression of diverse interests with efficient legislative procedure.

The First Bank of the United States, in Philadelphia, was chartered in 1791. The House of Representatives urged Alexander Hamilton to prepare an economic plan to provide loans for industrial development and assume the war debts of the states. Hamilton proposed a bank modeled after the Bank of England, with the right to establish branches in different regions of the country.

The early Congresses set a precedent for organizing House business by three means: establishment of rules governing the legislative process and debate, creation of an internal structure of committees and leadership positions, and the use of political parties to build legislative majorities. The Constitution granted the House complete authority over its own rules, and the members of the First Congress chose to follow the English parliamentary practices (including rules of conduct and debate) that the Continental Congress had used. The House also followed the English and colonial practice of forming committees to draft legislation. The House of Representatives set up standing (permanent) committees to deal with the heaviest areas of legislation, such as Interstate and Foreign Commerce, created in 1795, or Ways and Means (for tax and revenue bills), created in 1795 and made a standing committee in 1802. In these committees a small group of congressmen was able to efficiently draft a bill after the whole House had agreed to the measure in principle. By 1822,

The House Ways and Means Committee Hearing Room, U.S. Capitol, in 1959. The Ways and Means Committee was created in 1795 to study tax and revenue bills. Members of this standing committee are some of the most respected representatives in the House.

In an 18th-century Federalist cartoon, President Thomas Jefferson and the devil are depicted pulling down the government built by Washington and Adams. The Federalist Party, one of the first national political parties, criticized Jefferson and his administration and liked to picture him as a brandy-soaked anarchist.

the existing 21 standing committees, had been granted authority by the House to introduce legislation to the full body. The Speaker of the House was a position that had roots in the English House of Commons and the colonial assemblies; it evolved to provide its occupant with considerable control over House business. The first Speakers presided impartially over floor debates, but as politics became more partisan (party-oriented) after 1800, the Speakers began to wield such powers as the appointment of committee chairmen to influence the legislative process.

The most unexpected development in the early Congresses was the growth of political parties. In the 1790s the first two-party system in U.S. history grew out of congressional debates, particularly on foreign and fiscal policies. Divisions between northerners and southerners and between commercial and agricultural interests had emerged during the consideration of Hamilton's ambitious fiscal policy, one that included the creation of the national bank, advocated full payment of debts owed by the government, and established tariffs, or duties, that raised revenues and protected new industries. But organized parties in Congress appeared only with the consideration of foreign

The British attack on Washington, D.C., in 1814. Among the burned buildings were the White House, the Treasury Building, and the Capitol. After arguments between the war hawks and Federalists about American military preparation and finance threatened to divide Congress, the House decided to declare war on Great Britain in 1812.

policy after France and Great Britain went to war in 1793. The Federalists, who supported President Washington and Hamilton, favored a pro-British policy that encouraged investment and trade with the former mother country. James Madison led the congressional opposition that preferred an alliance with France and supported the agrarian-oriented foreign policy of Secretary of State Thomas Jefferson. In the House of Representatives, the Federalists and Jeffersonians (as the opposing party was called) organized informal caucuses, or closed political meetings, to plan legislative tactics and developed ties to partisan newspaper publishers and local political clubs. Most Americans, including most members of Congress, thought political parties were disruptive and hoped they would disappear after the turbulent early years of the government. After the Jeffersonians gained control of the Congress and

Jefferson was elected president in 1800, competition between these parties declined and the Federalists gradually disappeared. Congressional parties, however, had proved useful in organizing like-minded representatives and would repeatedly appear until they became an accepted and desired part of the structure of Congress.

The party ties that congressmen cultivated in their local districts with political societies and party newspapers were just one of the factors that made the House of Representatives the most important democratic forum in the country. The popular election of House members and regular reapportionment of House seats to reflect shifts in population also ensured that the House focused on the most important issues of the day. This was especially true during the two decades following 1810, during which Congress dominated the federal government. An aggressive group of congressmen, keen on expanding national power and promoting westward development, took charge of the House of Representatives in the years after 1810. The so-called war hawks, who entered the House in 1811, pushed for war with Great Britain in the hope of removing British restrictions on American commerce and eliminating Britain's claims on lands in the Northwest.

The most famous of the war hawks, and one of the most important members of the House ever, was Henry Clay of Kentucky. After a short term in the Sen-

Henry Clay was elected Speaker of the House in 1811. Clay led the war hawks, a congressional group that supported war with Great Britain and American expansion into Canada.

ate, Clay entered the House in 1811, at the age of 34, and was elected Speaker of the House on his first day. Clay took advantage of his position's control over the appointment of committee chairmen to place his allies in key positions of influence. Clay also made the Speaker the leader of the majority party. The number of standing committees grew from 10 in 1811 to 28 in 1825 as the House considered more and more complicated legislation. Clay and his followers promoted legislation to encourage the settlement of western lands and the development of domestic manufacturing. Clay's "American System" was designed to provide legislation favorable to each region of the country. As part of his plan, federal funding of canals and roads was appropriated to hasten settlement of the West and help southerners transport goods to market. A second Bank of the United States replaced the first Bank, when its charter expired in 1811, and offered credit to commercial traders and manufacturers in northeastern states as well as land speculators in the South and West. A high tariff on imported manufactures restricted the competition facing young industries in the East.

The House of Representatives had less influence over national politics after 1829, when the forceful Andrew Jackson became president, and such powerful men as Clay, John C. Calhoun, and Daniel Webster moved from the House to the Senate. The House remained an important forum for national issues, however.

In the years between 1820 and 1860 no issue was more divisive in the House or the nation than slavery. Early Congresses limited their discussion of the subject to the issue of the slave trade. Southern states depended on slave labor but the northern states did not. Until 1819, the nation had been equally divided between slave states and free states and neither side wished the other to gain a majority. Debate over the institution of slavery itself began in the House in 1819, when Congressman James Tallmadge, Jr., of New York offered an amendment that would have prohibited the importation of slaves into the newly formed state of Missouri. The House passed this amendment with the bill granting statehood to Missouri, while the Senate approved the statehood bill but rejected the Tallmadge amendment. The so-called Missouri Compromise was reached only when Speaker Clay convinced both houses to accept Missouri as a slave state but admit Maine as a free state and to exclude slavery from all other territory north of Missouri's southern border. For the time being Congress had dealt with the issue of slavery in the territories, but the significance of the Missouri debates was that the House and Senate had for the first time agreed to limit the expansion of slavery.

The House of Representatives found it difficult to avoid further discussion of slavery in the 1830s, when abolitionists (those who insisted on an immediate end to slavery) flooded Congress with petitions asking for the abolition of

Representatives Henry Clay, Daniel Webster, and John Calhoun were the House's most powerful orators during the 1820s. House prestige suffered when they accepted seats in the Senate: Webster in 1827, Clay in 1831, and Calhoun in 1832.

slavery in the District of Columbia. Since the 1790s, the House had adhered to a procedural rule that rejected all petitions pertaining to the slave trade. In 1836, John Quincy Adams began a frustrating campaign to introduce antislavery petitions. After leaving the presidency in 1829, Adams had entered the House of Representatives in 1831 and would spend 17 years there. Adams, the only former president to serve in the House, was an ardent opponent of slavery. His motion to consider the abolitionists' petitions prompted the House to pass the so-called gag rule that ordered all petitions dealing with slavery to be rejected without further consideration. Adams used his considerable parliamentary skills to present antislavery appeals, but the House repeatedly renewed the gag rule. Only in 1844, after the Democratic party split over the issue, did northern congressmen cross party lines to rescind the ban on abolitionists' petitions.

41

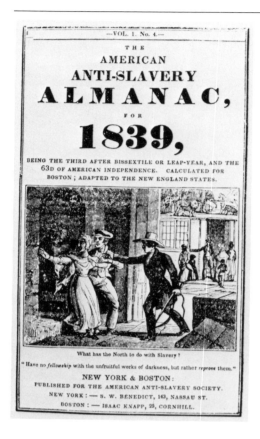

An 1839 almanac urges northerners to protect runaway slaves. In the 1830s, Congress passed a gag rule that forbade discussion of all antislavery petitions introduced in the House.

Despite the change in rules, most members of the House of Representatives continued to avoid a direct discussion of the future of slavery in America. Between the 1830s and 1850s, control of the House passed between the Whig party of Henry Clay and the Democratic party, which had elected Andrew Jackson president. (Republicans and Federalists who supported Jackson would later call themselves Democrats.) Both parties had popular support in both the North and the South and wanted to avoid a sectional division. The issue of slavery, however, was so fundamental to questions about national development that Congress could not entirely avoid it. A number of hotly contested races for Speaker of the House in the 1840s and 1850s revolved around expectations about how the candidates would deal with slavery. The House debated slavery most frequently when faced with the task of organizing western territory. In August 1846, during the Mexican War, the House appropriated funds for the organization of any territory won from Mexico. Attached to this funding bill was a proviso (a clause attaching a condition or restriction to a document), submitted by David Wilmot of Pennsylvania, that prohibited slavery in any new territory. The Senate refused to accept this condition, but the House attached the Wilmot Proviso to a bill organizing the Oregon Territory. The Thirtieth Congress, in which Abraham Lincoln served as a member of the House of Representatives, never passed the Wilmot Proviso as part of the various bills to which it was attached, but the divisions created by the debate over slavery in the territories threatened to bring congressional business to a standstill.

In 1850 the House agreed to a compromise on the issue of slavery worked out in the Senate. The Compromise of 1850 appeased southerners with a tough new law requiring the return of runaway slaves (the Fugitive Slave Law) and offered antislavery supporters the admission of California to the Union as a free state and the abolition of the slave trade in the District of Columbia. The illusion of peace lasted only until 1854, when Congress attempted to organize the

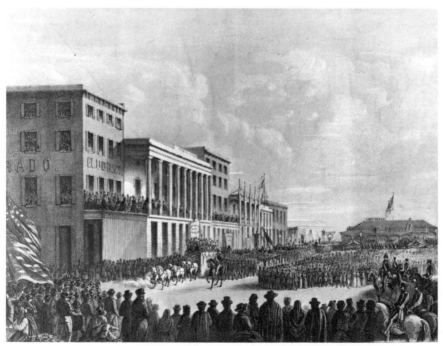

A parade in San Francisco commemorates California's admission to the Union in 1850. A congressional compromise on slavery admitted California as a free state and established a strict fugitive-slave law.

Kansas and Nebraska territories. The debate over slavery in the Kansas territory preoccupied Congress for several years. Ultimately legislators were unable to resolve the basic division between slave and free states. The political breakdown in Congress led to the collapse of the federal authority, the secession of 11 southern states, and the outbreak of the Civil War in 1861.

When the Southern states withdrew from the Union, the House of Representatives fell under the control of Northern congressmen, the majority of whom belonged to the recently formed Republican party. In the early months of the war, the Republican House and Senate worked easily with Republican president Lincoln in the mobilization of the military. The Republican congress-

Representative Preston Brooks of South Carolina beats Senator Charles Sumner of Massachusetts with his cane in 1856 in the Senate chamber, three days after Sumner's speech protesting slavery in Kansas. Hostilities between the North and South were mounting in the House and Senate.

A South Carolina ordinance proclaims the dissolution of the Union in 1860. While Congress continued to try to reach a compromise on the issue of slavery, the states prepared for war.

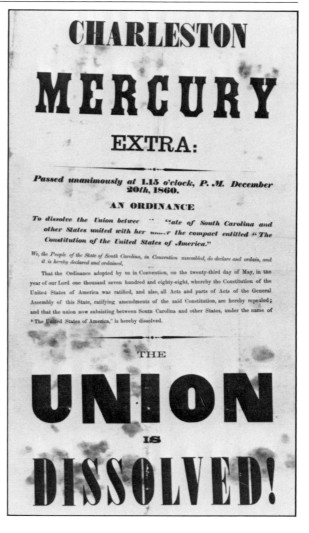

men, particularly the powerful group known as the Radicals, led by Thaddeus Stevens in the House and Charles Sumner in the Senate, came into conflict with the president when they planned for the reorganization and reconstruction of conquered Southern territory. The Radicals believed in the supremacy of Congress over all other branches of government, and they wanted full control over Reconstruction policy. Lincoln, however, had a strong enough personality to enforce his own policy of a quick readmittance to the Union for conquered Southern states.

President Andrew Johnson enraged the Radical Republicans when he vetoed their policies for Reconstruction in the Southern states. To exert control over the president, Congress passed the Tenure of Office Act, which prohibited him from removing civilian officials from office without the consent of the Senate.

After the assassination of Lincoln in 1865, his successor Andrew Johnson was no match for the well-organized and determined Radicals in Congress. The House and Senate easily overrode Johnson's vetoes and gained complete authority over Reconstruction policy. The most famous confrontation between the legislature and president came when the Congress passed the Tenure of Office Act in 1867. This act prevented Johnson from dismissing any cabinet officer without the approval of the Senate. Johnson considered the act unconstitutional and removed the secretary of war, Edwin Stanton, a close ally of congressional Radicals. By an overwhelming majority, the full House of Representatives voted for the only time in its history to impeach the president. In the Senate, which according to the Constitution tries any official impeached by the House, Johnson won acquittal by just one vote.

The Radical Republicans could be vindictive, as indicated by their attacks on Johnson, but they sincerely believed in the principle of congressional supremacy within the federal government. In carrying out their Reconstruction program they left an impressive legislative legacy. Passage of the Thirteenth (1864), Fourteenth (1866), and Fifteenth (1869) amendments to the Constitution by the House abolished slavery, extended federal authority to enforce civil rights against prohibitions by state governments, and guaranteed black men the right to vote. The Civil Rights acts of 1866 and 1875 guaranteed full citizenship to freed slaves and established an important precedent for the civil rights measures of the 20th century.

The enforcement of Congress's Reconstruction policy also made it possible for the first blacks to win election to the House and Senate. Hiram Revels of Mississippi became the first black in Congress when he was elected to the Senate in 1870. The first black member of the House of Representatives was Joseph Rainey of South Carolina. Rainey's election to the Forty-first Congress in 1870 was followed by the election of 19 other black Congressmen from southern states during the latter half of the 19th century. However, white

Some of the members of the 1868 House, which voted to impeach President Johnson. Thaddeus Stevens, seated second from the left, led the Radical Republicans, who opposed the president's policies.

southerners often feared the growing political influence of blacks and secured passage of state laws that excluded or discouraged blacks from voting. By the first decade of the 20th century, most southern states had effectively deprived blacks of the right to vote.

The reign of the Radical Republicans marked the beginning of a congressional domination of the federal government that lasted through the remainder of the 19th century. The House and Senate assumed unprecedented power in the areas of foreign relations and the country's rapid industrialization. The growth of large industry, the rise of large cities, and the growing number of immigrants created problems that many believed required federal regulation of the workplace and interstate commerce. Between Lincoln's presidency and that of Theodore Roosevelt, which began in 1901, no president was able to push through legislation to which Congress was opposed. The Senate was at the peak of its influence in the late 19th century, and the House also managed to increase its control over government policy. As Congress turned its attention to the Spanish-American War and later to the regulation of a growing economy,

An 1872 portrait of the first black representative, Joseph H. Rainey (second from right), and five black representatives and one senator in the Forty-first and Forty-second Congresses. Nearly two dozen blacks were elected to Congress in the late 1800s.

48

The U.S. Capitol was remodeled in the late 1850s to increase the size of the House and Senate chambers. The cast-iron dome and the two wings were completed in 1863.

the greater responsibilities of the House of Representatives, particularly in the area of federal spending, prompted an expansion of committees and their jurisdiction. The Ways and Means Committee had been responsible for all tax and spending bills since its creation as a select, or temporary, committee in 1795. In 1865 the House created an Appropriations Committee and a Committee on Banking and Currency in order to reduce the burden on Ways and Means. Other committees were formed to meet new problems in the post-Civil War era. The Committee on Education and Labor, formed in 1867, dealt with the problems of incorporating former slaves into a free society. The Committees on Mines and Mining (1865), Pacific Railroads (1865), Merchant Marine and Fisheries (1887),

Speaker Thomas B. Reed in 1891. Reed exerted so much control over the rules governing legislation that fellow congressmen nicknamed him "Czar Reed."

and Immigration and Naturalization (1893) considered the legislation relating to these important segments of the economy and American society.

The proliferation of committees and the independent power enjoyed by committee chairmen made the consideration of legislation a cumbersome and often inefficient process. The House's sheer growth in size also made it difficult to organize. The number of members in the House continued to grow as settlement spread to the Far West and immigrants swelled the nation's population. In the 1850s, when House membership reached 237, Congress decided to expand the Capitol building to include new chambers for the House and Senate and a proportionally larger dome over the center of the building. In 1857 the House moved into its present chamber; by 1863 the expansion was completed with the placement of a new cast-iron dome above the Capitol rotunda. Population growth and the apportionment of seats in the House

50

increased the number of representatives to 243 in 1860, 293 in 1870, and 332 in 1880.

The size of the House of Representatives and the expanded legislative role of committees made it difficult for any Speaker of the House to gain control of House business. In the years following the Civil War, Speakers such as Republican James G. Blaine of Maine and Democrat Samuel J. Randall of Pennsylvania appointed as chairmen to committees those who supported their legislative programs. Although Clay recognized the political advantages of naming his supporters to lead committees, most earlier Speakers had generally granted committee chairs to the members with the longest record of service, regardless of party affiliation. Since 1858 the Speaker had also served as chairman of the Rules Committee, which determined when bills came to the floor for consideration and established the regulations governing debate on particular measures. Through stricter control of the Rules Committee, Speakers were able to limit the time for debate and prevent the opposition from blocking legislation with technical points of order, thereby speeding up passage of their legislative programs.

Yet no one gained thorough control over the legislative process until 1889, when Thomas Reed of Maine was elected Speaker. The Republican leader quickly became known as "Czar Reed" because of his authoritarian use of the rules to stifle all parliamentary obstacles to the majority party's wishes. Reed also changed the rules to make it easier for members to introduce legislation and reduced the number of members in the quorum required for floor action— the full House's debate and vote on a bill. When the Democrats regained control of the House in 1891, the new Speaker of the House, Charles Crisp of Georgia, continued to use Reed's efficient, if authoritarian, rules.

During the last third of the 19th century, control of the House swung back and forth between Republicans and Democrats. The differences dividing the congressional parties revolved around the government's role in an ever-more-complex industrial economy. The most controversial business of the House in these years concerned technical questions about the proper level of tariffs on imported goods and the supply of money in circulation. At the heart of these debates were questions of how the government might best stimulate economic growth and who should benefit from the mixed effects of that growth.

During a serious depression in the 1890s, a growing number of congressmen advocated government programs to regulate the power of new corporations and to provide social welfare for the disadvantaged. A new third party, the Populists, or People's party, elected a number of congressmen who demanded some protection for farmers who were forced to pay high transportation costs charged by unregulated railroads and who were dependent on credit from private banks. The Progressive Republicans—those Republicans who championed reform and opposed the conservative members of the Republican party—and Democrats in Congress also supported more aggressive economic regulation. After 1901 the support of President Theodore Roosevelt encouraged Progressives in the House but was not enough to overcome the rigid leadership of the Speaker.

Joseph Gurney Cannon of Illinois was Speaker from 1903 to 1911. An opponent of progressive legislation, Cannon ruled the House as autocratically as any of his predecessors. His strict control of the Rules Committee prevented even his fellow Republicans from getting legislation to the floor if he opposed it. A coalition of Progressive Republicans and Democrats made several attempts to change the rules so as to allow one day a week when bills could come to the floor without the permission of the Rules Committee. These and other challenges failed until 1910, when a large majority of the House agreed to drastically reduce the powers of the Speaker. Upon the adoption of the resolution submitted by George Norris of Nebraska, the Speaker no longer had control over the appointment of committee chairmen and was removed from the Rules Committee. "Uncle Joe" Cannon, as House members referred to him, lost the speakership in 1911, when Democrats took control of the House. Cannon continued as a representative in Congress until his retirement in 1923, after 46 years of service.

With the decline of the Speaker's authority, party organization became a more important means of directing the legislative process. When the Democrats took over as the majority party in 1911, they used the party caucus (closed meeting of party members) to name the party leadership and plan strategy on particular bills. Each party now selected a Committee on Committees that made all committee assignments for members of that party. The ratio of seats granted to the majority and minority parties was determined by the leaders of the majority party. Much of the power formerly in the hands of the Speaker now went to the majority leader, who controlled party action on the floor of the House.

When the Republicans regained control of the House in 1919, they organized their party conference after the model of the Democratic caucus. Parties became a more effective means of organization in the 20th century in part because there was a greater continuity of service among the members of the House. Throughout the 19th century, turnover was so high that in the 1870s more than half the congressmen elected in a given year were freshmen. By 1900 only 30 percent were freshmen, and the rate of turnover has declined

President Woodrow Wilson addresses Congress in 1916. A Democrat, he worked closely with a Democratic majority in both houses to enact legislation controlling corporate monopolies, reorganizing banking, and lowering tariffs on iron and steel.

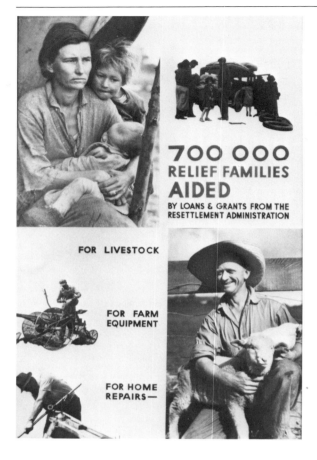

A display illustrates achievements of the Resettlement Administration, one of the federal agencies created in 1935 by New Deal legislation. Working with Congress, the agency gave financial aid to farm families and built model suburban homes.

700 000
RELIEF FAMILIES
AIDED
BY LOANS & GRANTS FROM THE
RESETTLEMENT ADMINISTRATION

FOR LIVESTOCK

FOR FARM
EQUIPMENT

FOR HOME
REPAIRS—

throughout the 20th century as Americans have found a career in the federal government more attractive than it was earlier, when the government exercised less influence over national affairs.

The presidency of Democrat Woodrow Wilson (1913–21) further encouraged party organization and provided a new role for the legislative leadership. As a scholar, Wilson had published a book entitled *Congressional Government* in 1885. Wilson thought Congress and the president should work in unison, much as the prime minister and Parliament in Great Britain jointly developed legislative programs. When he entered the White House in 1913, he established an unprecedentedly close relationship with the Democratic leadership in Congress. Wilson also revived the practice of delivering the State of the Union message, an annual speech to Congress in which the president proposes his legislative program. All presidents since Thomas Jefferson (including Jefferson) had sent a written message. The result of Wilson's relationship with his fellow Democrats on Capitol Hill was quick passage of such major legislation as the Clayton Anti-Trust Act (which gave the federal government new power to limit corporate monopolies, or companies that have exclusive control over some product or service) the Federal Reserve Act (which reformed banking and currency policies), and the Federal Trade Commission Act (which granted the federal government authority to restrict unfair trade practices).

Although Republicans controlled the White House and the Congress in the 1920s, no president followed Wilson's pattern of working closely with the Congress. In part this was due to the lack of any comprehensive legislative program from either the White House or the Republican leadership in Congress, both of which were content with the operation of the economy in the 1920s. The major development in that decade related to the structure of the House rather than any significant legislation. Since the 1790s the House had expanded its membership as the nation's population grew. The addition of new members had made it possible to reapportion House seats without depriving any states of existing seats. When the Census Committee recommended the addition of 53 seats following the census of 1920, the House instead voted to limit membership to 435. The House has not added any permanent seats since the 1920s, but has reapportioned the 435 seats to reflect population changes.

The economic depression that began in 1929 created popular demands for more governmental recovery programs than Republican president Herbert Hoover or Congress was willing to endorse. The return of a Democratic majority in 1931 and the election of Franklin Roosevelt to the presidency in 1932 initiated a new relationship between the executive branch and Congress. Roosevelt worked closely with the Democratic majority in both houses during the first months of his administration. During the 100-day session that opened the Seventy-third Congress in 1933, the House and Senate passed legislation that initiated the New Deal program of economic recovery and social welfare. Roosevelt received, and would continue to enjoy, strong support from many members of Congress, but the tremendous expansion of executive authority needed to carry out New Deal programs gave the presidency new power that the Congress could not equal. The president's authority over the mobilization for World War II further enhanced the executive branch's domination of the federal government. The expansion of the executive branch was so great under Roosevelt that it resulted in a permanent redistribution of power between the president and Congress. Future presidents played a greater role in the initiation of legislation and held authority over the expansion of federal programs.

In the hope that a more efficient legislature would be better able to deal with a powerful executive, Congress launched a major reform of both internal structure and procedure. The Legislative Reorganization Act of 1946 created the outline of the modern House as it operates today. However, the resulting changes in the budget process, whereby the House and Senate agreed to develop an overall budget before considering specific appropriations, and the consolidation of committees did little to resolve the conflict between congressional and executive authority.

A crowd jams the caucus room during a hearing of the House Committee on Un-American Activities in 1948. Democratic party menbers bers who had earlier opposed President Roosevelt's policies used the HUAC as an arena for their attacks and charged the Truman administration with sympathizing with communists.

Since World War II, Congress has fought the expanded power of the presidency. The struggle began with President Harry Truman, who came to power in 1945, at the time that Soviet-American distrust was solidifying, and was bent on proving himself a strong president. He denounced Soviet aggression after the war and tried to extend many of the New Deal measures established by the Roosevelt administration. Despite his attempt to win passage of liberal legislation, such as the extension of social security benefits, an increase in the minimum wage, construction of subsidized low-income housing, and granting the president power to cope with inflation, bipartisan conservatives in Congress fought with Truman over most of his proposals and passed only the housing bill. As a result, Truman spent his final months in office fighting a congressional opposition that wished to repeal New Deal programs and focusing on the war in Korea.

The House Committee on Un-American Activities and the Chambers-Hiss Case

The House Committee on Un-American Activities (HUAC) was a special committee formed in 1938 to investigate alleged communists whose activities were considered a threat to American democracy. During the 1930s, many Americans supported the Communist, Nazi, and Fascist parties of the Soviet Union, Germany, and Italy by giving money, making trade agreements, and helping to publicize those parties' views in the United States. HUAC originally intended to put a stop to communist propaganda, but it actually focused its attention on a wide variety of artists, intellectuals, labor leaders, and other so-called liberals who were considered to have unorthodox views at the time.

In 1945, when a raid on the magazine *Amerasia* turned up a large quantity of classified State Department documents, HUAC was ordered to investigate the loyalty of civil servants. HUAC's investigation of alleged communists in the State Department culminated in its famous hearings of 1948, which implicated Alger Hiss, president of the Carnegie Endowment for International Peace and a former State Department official who had coordinated foreign policy.

Elizabeth Bentley, an agent for communist groups in Washington, D.C., and New York in the early 1940s, testified at the HUAC hearings. Bentley named several government officials as Communists but presented little evidence to back her accusations. While seeking someone who could support Bentley's claims, HUAC discovered *Time* magazine editor Whittaker Chambers, a self-confessed courier for communist groups with ties to Bentley's organization. Chambers also appeared before HUAC and during his testimony named nine Communist associates, many of whom had served in the Roosevelt and Truman administrations. One of the most prestigious members of this group was Alger Hiss.

The House committee quickly issued subpoenas to the accused, hoping to find the person who had given Chambers the State Department documents. Some denied the allegations; others pleaded the Fifth Amendment, refusing to answer questions on the grounds that they might incriminate themselves. But because his career had been seriously jeopardized by Chambers's accusations, Alger Hiss was willing to respond to the charges made against him.

Hiss was a convincing witness during HUAC's questioning, denying all connections with the Communist party. However, California representative Richard M. Nixon noticed that Hiss responded evasively to the question of whether or not he knew Chambers. Suspicious of Hiss's testimony, Nixon questioned Chambers again in private sessions, during which Chambers revealed details of Hiss's personal life, indicating that he had indeed known Hiss at one time.

Chambers repeated his charge that Hiss was a member of the Communist party, and Hiss met

Representative Richard Nixon (right) of California and a colleague examine a portion of the microfilm surrendered as evidence in the Hiss-Chambers case.

Chambers's challenge by suing him for slander. Tensions in the HUAC mounted.

Cleverly, Chambers made his move to strengthen the case against Hiss. For 10 years he kept an envelope containing State Department documents, memos from Hiss, and undeveloped microfilm. He recovered the envelope from a dumbwaiter shaft in Brooklyn, New York, and handed over most of this material to the U.S. Justice Department. Still planning to defend his testimony, but at a later time, Chambers hid the microfilm inside a hollowed-out pumpkin on his Maryland farm.

The Justice Department needed further proof that Hiss had given the classified documents to Chambers. Desperate for additional evidence, Nixon subpoenaed Chambers. In a scene claiming all the drama of a Hollywood movie, Chambers surrendered the microfilm. It provided the HUAC with proof of Hiss's association with Chambers and eventually led to Hiss's conviction for the crime of perjury, or lying under oath.

Nixon told the press that Hiss's indictment indisputably justified the need for congressional investigations of subversives. The Chambers-Hiss case set the stage for the infamous Senate hearings during which Chairman Joseph McCarthy investigated communist sympathizers during the 1950s.

In the latter half of the 20th century, with the fear of nuclear conflict inspiring avoidance of declared war and increased security, Congress has allowed the presidency greater control over foreign policy. Following a reported attack by North Vietnam on American ships, Congress, in the Tonkin Gulf Resolution of 1964, gave President Lyndon Johnson special authority to carry out military action in Vietnam without a declaration of war. The resolution allowed the president "to take all necessary measures to repel any armed attack against the forces of the United States to prevent further aggression." Presidents Johnson and Richard Nixon then continued to commit troops to Vietnam without gaining further approval of Congress. However, the prolonged military involvement in Southeast Asia convinced a majority of congressmen to pass, over presidential veto, the War Powers Act of 1973. This act required the president to report to Congress on any use of American military forces abroad. The act of 1973 also limited troop commitment to 60 days unless Congress declared war or issued a specific authorization. Since the Vietnam War, both the House and Senate have more closely supervised the executive branch's conduct of all foreign policy.

Congress faced another conflict with the White House during the Watergate scandal of President Nixon's administration. A burglary at the Democratic party's national headquarters at the Watergate complex in Washington, D.C., in June 1972 brought charges of involvement by the executive branch and a cover-up by the president himself. After a prolonged investigation by a Senate committee chaired by Senator Sam Ervin in February 1974, the House of Representatives ordered its Judiciary Committee, chaired by Representative Peter Rodino, to explore grounds for the impeachment of the president. The investigation disclosed evidence of criminal activity (illegal wiretapping, illegal campaign contributions, and income tax evasion) and revealed the existence of tape recordings of conversations Nixon had secretly made in the Oval Office. The Watergate prosecutors fought to gain control of the tapes, believing that the conversations would confirm that Nixon was guilty of obstructing justice. Nixon refused to turn over the tapes, even after receiving a subpoena (a court order requiring a person to produce specific documents), until receiving a Supreme Court order. After reviewing the contents of the tapes—which were allegedly altered by Nixon or his aides—and after conducting nationally televised hearings, the House's Judiciary Committee voted three articles of impeachment against the president: obstruction of justice, abuse of presidential power, and refusal to obey House subpoenas. Nixon resigned from office on August 9, 1974, before the full House could vote on impeachment.

Antiwar protesters at the 1968 Democratic National Convention in Chicago. Millions of Americans attacked the U.S. government for its involvement in the Vietnam War. One victim of the antiwar attitude was President Lyndon B. Johnson, who decided not to seek the nomination for another term.

Chairman Peter Rodino (left) of the House Judiciary Committee presided over the 1974 impeachment hearings investigating President Richard Nixon's involvement in the political scandal known as Watergate.

The question of the proper distribution of authority between Congress and the presidency remained unsettled in the aftermath of Watergate. President Jimmy Carter enjoyed a Democratic majority in both houses of Congress, but he and his staff had little experience dealing with Capitol Hill and often alienated the leadership of their own party. Republican Ronald Reagan initially found great support in the House, despite the Democratic majority. Like earlier presidents, however, Reagan also faced serious conflicts with Congress over the control of foreign policy. Through the appropriations process, the Democratic-controlled House tried to restrict Reagan's power, particularly in regard to U.S. policy in Central America. The so-called Iran-Contra Affair dominated the news media from the fall of 1986 through most of 1987. Across the nation, Americans heard and read about disclosures of arms sales to Iran that turned into an arrangement to free American hostages in Lebanon. The profits from the sales of the weapons were to be diverted to aid Nicaraguan rebels, called the Contras. Investigations by the Tower Commission, a panel set up by the White House and headed by former senator John Tower of Texas, found many weaknesses in Reagan's administrative approach but did not propose structural changes. A joint House-Senate investigating committee conducted hearings during the summer of 1987 and unearthed serious abuses of the American system of government by several officials; however, there was no evidence to contradict Reagan's assertion that he did not know about the covert (secret) diversion of arms-sales profits to the Contras. After the investigation of the Iran-Contra Affair, Reagan told Congress that he would revise his secret-operations policy and would inform Congress within 48 hours of the onset of most major activities.

Both houses of Congress and the president are elected to pursue together the concerns of the American people. The House of Representatives continues to struggle to find an effective means of responding to the enormous power of the executive branch.

Lieutenant Colonel Oliver North takes an oath prior to testifying before the Select Committee on Secret Military Assistance to Iran and the Nicaraguan Opposition (Iran-Contra Committee) in 1987. Both House and Senate members explored the covert actions that were taken by the Reagan administration without congressional approval.

A representative walks past the Members Only sign to enter the House chamber. Since the First Congress met in 1789, House membership has increased from 59 to 435.

FOUR

The Modern House of Representatives

As the House of Representatives approaches its 200th anniversary, it is a vastly more complex institution than the one that first convened in New York City in 1789. The constitutional role assigned to the House of Representatives has grown as the nation has expanded its population and territory. In addition to changing in scale, the House has evolved to meet the need for more complicated legislation. It has also changed as the balance of power has shifted between the two houses of Congress and among the legislative, judicial, and executive branches of the government.

Some changes in the government have altered the unique constitutional character of the House of Representatives. Because the ratification of the Seventeenth Amendment to the Constitution in 1913 decreed the popular election of senators, House members are not the only government officeholders subject to direct election. As the conduct of foreign affairs became more important in the 20th century, the Senate's broader jurisdiction in that area began to overshadow the influence of the House of Representatives. Expansion of the presidency has made the executive branch at least as important a link between the federal government and local communities as is the House. Often an apprehensive public, dissatisfied with programs that do not work and policies that do not measure up to the urgent needs of the moment, will look to the president to provide strong leadership.

Despite these threats to its traditional prerogatives, the House of Representatives has maintained the most important aspects of its constitutional role. Proportional representation and frequent elections have kept the House the branch of government most representative of the people's views. The exclusive authority to originate all revenue and spending bills gives the House an important advantage in working out legislation with the Senate. The power to initiate the annual appropriation of government funds also provides an effective check on the power of the executive branch. In the years since World War II, House committees have assumed the right to oversee the operation of federal programs in the executive branch.

In order to understand how the House of Representatives carries out its constitutional mandate it is necessary to explore the internal structure that allows members to translate popular concerns into a workable legislative program. Today, 435 members represent 50 states. Since the 1920s, when the House established a limit on membership, the reapportionment of seats after each census (every ten years) has taken seats away from some states and increased the size of other state delegations. Over the past 50 years the greatest losses have come to states in the Mid-Atlantic region and the Midwest. The delegation from New York, for more than a century the largest, declined from 45 seats in 1940 to 34 in 1980. Old industrial states such as Pennsylvania and Illinois have suffered comparable losses. The growth of such states as Florida and Texas has enabled the South to increase slightly its representation in the years since 1930. The greatest gains in House seats have been in the Far West. California, now the largest state delegation with 45 members, gained 25 seats between 1930 and 1980. In addition to the 435 voting members of the House, the District of Columbia and the U.S. Territories, such as Guam and Puerto Rico, each elect a delegate to Congress. These delegates serve on committees and can vote in the committees, but cannot vote on the floor of the House.

The two-year term of representatives helps ensure that the House responds regularly to popular opinion, just as the decennial (every 10 years) reapportionment, after the census of the population is taken, has allowed the House to reflect shifts in population. The tremendous expense of modern elections and the need for extended campaigns have led some political scientists and others to propose a term of four years for House members. Representatives, however, have rejected such proposals in the belief that the two-year term helps distinguish this body from other government institutions. The two-year term means that each House is a separate body, unlike the Senate, which is a continuing body, with only one-third of its members running for reelection every two years. After each election, the new House elects a new leadership and approves the rules that will govern its business. In the House, one Congress cannot do anything to bind a later Congress. (A Congress lasts for two years, beginning in January of the year following the biennial election of members, and is divided into two sessions.) As the framers of the Constitution intended, the independence of each Congress makes the House of Representatives more directly responsive to the people than is the Senate.

House members are elected from districts of equal population within their states. In the 19th and early 20th centuries some states voted for a slate of candidates to represent the whole state. By the 1960s the Supreme Court ruled that district elections were the only means by which all voters could be equally represented. Voter turnout for House elections is lowest in the off-year elections that fall between presidential elections. During the past 50 years no off-year election has attracted more than 45 percent of registered voters. If a House member dies in office or retires before the end of the term, voters have an opportunity to choose a successor in a special election called by the state governor. In contrast, when a Senate seat is vacated, the state governor selects a replacement without a popular election.

Since the late 19th century, the great majority of representatives elected to Congress have been members of either the Democratic or Republican party. The strength and the continuity of these two parties, after the fluctuating party competition in the first 100 years of Congress's history, have made the parties' organization an integral part of the structure of the House of Representatives. Throughout the 20th century the rules governing the legislative process have been based on the presence of two major political parties.

The Congressional Caucus

The central organization of the House parties is the caucus. Congressional caucuses originated in the Jeffersonian period but did not become an important part of the House operations until 1890, when Speaker Thomas Reed revived the caucus as a means of carrying out the Republicans' legislative programs. Today the caucus is seldom used to enforce party loyalty on a specific vote, but it remains the organization in which each party maps out its strategy. After

Democratic caucus members convening in the House chamber in 1963. Caucuses of both parties establish a legislative platform, or program, each year and elect floor leaders and party whips.

each election, the Democratic Caucus and the Republican Conference (as that party's caucus was renamed in 1911) gather all the members from their respective parties to elect the party leadership for that Congress. The Speaker of the House is officially elected in a vote of all House members, but since the advent of political parties the majority party's caucus agrees on its candidate for Speaker before the vote on the House floor. Election by the caucus also makes the Speaker the head of the majority party as well as the presiding officer of the House, as prescribed by the Constitution. Each caucus elects a floor leader (called the majority leader or minority leader depending on the party's status), who organizes his or her party's response to certain bills when they are brought before the full House, and party whips, assistant floor leaders who work with the party members to organize the vote on individual bills.

As the majority party in the House since 1955, the Democrats have used their caucus to revise House rules and initiate broader participation of younger and newer members in the legislative process. Since 1974, the Democratic Caucus has added to its power by assuming authority to elect committee chairmen. Previously, the Democratic members of the Committee on Ways and Means selected as chairman the committee member with the longest term of service. In 1973 the Democratic Caucus created a Steering and Policy Committee that allowed a broad group of party members to influence the party's program. This committee is made up of the elected leadership and 12 regionally elected members, as well as 8 others appointed by the Speaker. The Steering and Policy Committee, with a total of 24 members, devises a comprehensive legislative strategy for each Congress. The Republican Policy Committee serves a similar role for that party, but is less closely tied to the leadership.

The Speaker of the House

Despite the expanded role of the party caucus in recent years, party leadership remains the most important influence on the legislative program. As leader of the majority party and presiding officer, the Speaker of the House has authority over the referral of bills to committees and the application of House rules. In the 20th century, Speakers have not held the complete control of rules and appointment of committee chairmen that was enjoyed by Thomas Reed and Joseph Cannon. The modern Speaker has instead needed to use his position as presiding officer to develop the power of persuasion. Nicholas Longworth, a very popular and courtly Speaker from 1925 to 1931, met informally with his fellow party members and relied on his powers of persuasion to manage the Republican party's legislative program. Sam Rayburn, whose tenure as Speaker of the House was the longest in history, expanded on Longworth's model. As Speaker for all but four years between 1940 and 1961, Rayburn, with little of the institutional authority held by Reed or Cannon, became perhaps the most effective legislative strategist in the history of the House. Rayburn's advice to young congressmen was "to get along, go along," and those who showed party loyalty were rewarded. Since the reforms of the 1970s placed greater power in the majority caucus and the Steering and Policy Committee, a Speaker's personal style has become more important than ever.

Sam Rayburn, whose tenure as Speaker of the House (1940–47; 1949–53; 1955–61) was the longest in history, persuaded members of his party to adopt proposals by meeting with them informally to discuss the issues.

The Majority and Minority Leaders

The Speaker must work closely with the majority leader, who directs the day-to-day management of the party's legislative program. The majority leader, who usually becomes Speaker upon the latter's retirement, works closely with committee chairmen to report bills, or sends out the findings and recommendations to the full House, and has authority to arrange the legislative schedule on the floor of the House. The minority leader, who is that party's candidate for Speaker, plays a similar role with the minority members on committees and organizes the defense against the majority party's legislation. The minority leader, however, has no authority to schedule debate on particular legislation.

The Committees and Their Chairmen

Most of the business of the House of Representatives takes place not in sessions on the floor of the House chamber but rather in the committees. Congressional committees, like political parties, have no basis in the Constitution, but they have nevertheless become the most important means of developing legislation for consideration by the full House of Representatives. The standing committees, which have authority to submit legislation, were established to give specialized attention to areas in need of regular congressional action. As the work of Congress became more complicated and demanding in the 19th century, the House established more and more of these committees. By 1913 the House had 61 standing committees. The Legislative Reorganization Act of 1946 eliminated some committees and consolidated others in order to streamline the consideration of proposed legislation. The number of House committees was reduced from 45 to 19, and their jurisdictions were brought in line to complement the modern organization of the executive branch. The current committees established or left intact by the Legislative Reorganization Act of 1946 are Agriculture, Appropriations, Armed Services, Banking, District of Columbia, Education and Labor, Energy and Commerce, Finance and Urban Affairs, Foreign Affairs, Government Operations, House Administration, Interior and Insular Affairs, Judiciary, Merchant Marine and Fisheries, Post Office and Civil Service, Public Works and Transportation, Rules, Veterans' Affairs, and Ways and Means. In 1975 the House abolished the Committee on Internal Security, known in 1946 as the Un-American Activities Committee. In more recent years the House has established the

71

Tip O'Neill:
Speaker of the House (1977–86)

On October 18, 1986, at the closing session of the Ninety-ninth Congress, Thomas P. "Tip" O'Neill stepped down as Speaker of the United States House of Representatives, concluding a decade in which he had served as both leader and champion of the House. His term as Speaker was the longest continuous term in congressional history and capped a remarkable political career.

During his 35 years as a U.S. representative from Massachusetts, O'Neill developed a reputation as a strong and devoted leader of the Democratic party. He carefully kept abreast of issues that concerned his constituents back home, often reiterating his belief that "all politics is local."

The son of a Cambridge, Massachusetts, city councilman, O'Neill graduated from Boston College in 1936, where he was voted "class politician." That fall he was elected to a seat in the Massachusetts State House of Representatives.

O'Neill moved up quickly in the State House hierarchy. In 1946 he was voted state minority leader, and after mapping out a 1947 campaign strategy that won the Massachusetts Democrats a majority in the House for the first time in more than a century, he was elected State House Speaker. He used his power to aid mental health programs, increase financial benefits to the elderly, and provide housing for veterans.

In 1952, O'Neill was elected to the U.S. House of Representatives. When he returned to the House for his second term, in 1955, he was appointed to the prestigious Rules Committee. He later commented: "Looking back, I can see that serving on the Rules Committee was an important key to my future power in the House. Most of my fellow members of Congress were on committees that specialized in one particular area. But as a member of the Rules Committee, I had a general knowledge of every piece of legislation that came down the pike. I also came into contact with almost every member of the House, because no matter what kind of legislation was

Speaker of the House Thomas "Tip" O'Neill—acting as presiding officer of the House—raises his gavel to begin legislative proceedings.

being considered, both its advocates and its opponents would come to us with their arguments."

During the 1950s and 1960s, House politics was dominated by an unofficial seniority system that required less experienced members to wait their turn before filling important positions. O'Neill worked within these constraints, remaining loyal to his district and the Democratic party. In 1970 he was rewarded for his staunchness with appointment as party whip; soon after he revised the method by which the House Democrats were informed about current issues and upcoming legislation, establishing weekly meetings that were attended by both senior and junior members. The Democratic party was strengthened and communication between House leaders, members, and their constituents was vastly improved. O'Neill's hard work did not go unnoticed. In 1973 his Democratic colleagues elected him to the critical position of House majority leader and, in 1977, Speaker of the House.

O'Neill's first challenge as Speaker was to restore the country's faith in its political leaders, a faith that had been damaged by the Watergate scandal of the Nixon administration. To regain the public's trust, O'Neill pushed through the Rules Committee a tough ethics bill. Although unpopular with members of Congress because it imposed limitations on their outside earnings, the Ethics in Government Act of 1978 helped win back the public's confidence and strengthened O'Neill's position as a party leader.

As Speaker, O'Neill encouraged change in House procedures and structure. In 1974 he had had to adjust to a transformed House membership when 118 Democrats, nicknamed "Watergate babies," were elected, defeating some of the old guardians of the House system. These new members were determined to phase out the seniority system and succeeded in increasing their own power by creating many new committees. O'Neill labored to keep his party united—he reined in the tenacious junior members and placated the stubborn senior members—and kept the House system working effectively.

In 1979 O'Neill agreed to allow television coverage in the House, providing the public with a closer view of the legislative process.

But O'Neill's greatest tests came during his courageous battles with the Reagan administration. O'Neill often disagreed with Reagan's social policies and found his programs insensitive to the poor. He fought Reagan's budget reductions, such as those in Social Security benefits, college education loans, and in children's nutrition programs. Looking back, he remembered these years as the toughest of his career: "I certainly hadn't become Speaker to dismantle the programs I had fought for all my life. When the Reagan plan got going in 1981, I saw myself as Horatio at the bridge. Somebody had to stand out there and maintain the basic creed of the Democratic party, which has always believed that we are responsible for the welfare of our fellow Americans."

Committees on Science and Technology (1958), Small Business (1975), and Budget (1975). There are currently 22 standing committees in the House.

The party caucuses have been responsible for committee assignments since the House deprived the Speaker of that authority in 1910. In the Republican Conference, committee assignments are handed out by a Committee on Committees, which has a member from each state with a Republican representative. Since 1974, the Democratic Steering and Policy Committee has had the power to make committee assignments for that party. Committee assignments can be the most important determinant of a member's success in Congress. Accordingly, party leaders use their power of appointment as an element of influence with individual members. The party in the majority at the opening of each Congress determines the ratio of party members on each committee.

The House periodically establishes other types of committees that do not have the authority to report legislation. Select and special committees are created to investigate a specific issue or carry out a certain job, respectively, whether it be a simple problem of administration or a serious crisis in the government. These committees expire at the end of a Congress, although in recent years the Select Committee on Aging has been renewed in every succeeding Congress. Because it is a select committee, members are allowed to serve on the Committee on Aging without losing their seats on more powerful committees. Joint committees are usually temporary and bring together senators and representatives to study certain issues of common interest such as the Library of Congress or the Government Printing Office.

Throughout the history of Congress, the committee chairman has been a powerful figure who has the ability to determine what legislation will reach the floor of the House. For much of the 20th century, the position of chairman was particularly influential because of the strict observance of the seniority system. After Speakers lost the power to appoint chairmen, the party in power awarded the position to the member with the most years of service on the committee. As long as seniority determined leadership, the chairman was secure to run the committee as he pleased. Beginning in the late 1960s, a large number of young Democrats were elected to the House and challenged the system that denied them influence in committees. By 1974 these Democrats secured a number of party reforms, including the secret-ballot election of committee chairmen. The following year the Democratic Caucus refused to give chairmanships to the senior members of three committees. The reforms of 1974 officially killed the seniority system, but in most cases the majority caucus has continued to

A House committee holds a hearing to investigate whether the health of American veterans was harmed by exposure to the defoliant Agent Orange during the Vietnam War. Committees question witnesses and conduct extensive research before submitting their conclusions to the full House.

delegate the chairmanship to the senior committee member. As a result of this reform, the committee chairman, like the modern Speaker, maintains his power through persuasion rather than the institutional force of his office.

The House Staff

The modern House of Representatives carries out its business with the aid of a variety of support offices. Since the First Congress, the Clerk of the House, elected by the members, has kept the records and journal of House proceedings

A congressional staff at work in a Washington, D.C., office. A representative will often seek assistance from aides in preparing reports on pending legislation.

and served as the chief administrative officer. The sergeant at arms is the staff member in charge of the doorkeepers and press galleries. He is also the law-enforcement and protocol officer. Perhaps the most important, and least recognized, of the House offices is the Parliamentarian, who is not a member of the House. Named by the Speaker, but usually serving throughout changes in the leadership or party control, the Parliamentarian serves as an adviser on legislative procedure. His or her thorough knowledge of precedents and House rules gives this officer extraordinary influence with members who want to know how to get a bill before a certain committee or brought to the floor under the most advantageous circumstances.

In addition to these staff members, there are several other offices that serve Congress; for example, those that assist in research when legislation is considered and make sure that the Capitol building is well maintained. The Library of Congress was created in 1800 to purchase books for use by Congress and now serves the needs of both houses, the president, state and local governments, and the public. It is a vast collection of publications, official documents, and records that provides House members with the reference material they need to complete research on legislative proposals. The Congressional Research Service, a division of the Library of Congress, is a staff agency that assists members in studying their proposals.

The Congressional Budget Office, established in 1974, provides Congress with basic data about the annual federal budget, including economic forecasting and analyses of economic trends in the nation. It monitors the results of congressional action on appropriations and revenue bills and compares them against the targets or ceilings specified by Congress. It also furnishes the House and Senate Budget committees with an annual report about spending and revenues among major programs and takes into account the development and needs of the nation.

The Architect of the Capitol, originally appointed by President Washington in 1793 to plan and construct the Capitol building, supervises the care and maintenance of the Capitol, the U.S. Supreme Court building, Library of Congress buildings, and the House office buildings (Cannon House Office Building, Longworth House Office Building, and the Rayburn House Office Building). The Architect also makes arrangements with the proper authorities for ceremonies held in the Capitol and on the grounds.

The tremendous load of legislation and constituent case work (the work representatives do for residents of their districts—for instance, answering letters and giving tours) in a modern House office has contributed to an expansion of congressional staff during the past 40 years. In 1893, members of the House were allowed only one clerk and as late as 1946 individual members could hire no more than five assistants. By the 1980s, however, each member's office could employ as many as 18 full-time employees, and committee staffs had grown from 167 in 1947 to nearly 2,000. In 1987 the entire House of Representatives employed nearly 12,000 people. The current House is a large operation in need of food-service workers, building-maintenance teams, and even its own police force.

The most important source of expansion has been the changes in the organization and business of the House of Representatives. The Legislative Reorganization Act of 1946 reduced the number of committees but increased

In 1916, Jeannette Rankin of Montana became the first woman elected to the House. As a representative, Rankin worked to achieve national suffrage (the right to vote) for women. Since her election, more than 100 women have served as representatives.

the need for committee staff. Committee staffs have become responsible for preparing reports on the increasing volume of legislation passing through the consolidated committees. In a variety of tasks, only staff members can provide the expertise required for specialized legislation. The volume and complexity of legislation has also prompted the expansion of the members' personal staffs. The representative's staff, one-third of which works in the district office rather than in Washington, D.C., handles requests from constituents and special-interest groups such as business, farm, and veterans' organizations. Members of Congress in post–World War II years have used their staff to produce independent research in order to avoid reliance on the information provided by the executive branch.

Career Congressmen

The members of the House have themselves developed greater expertise on legislative matters as their average term served in Congress has lengthened. The 20th century has seen the rise of the career congressman who serves for several terms and sees the House as an end in itself. In the 19th century the great majority of congressmen served only one or two terms before returning to private life or political office in their states. In part, improved transportation has made it possible for members of Congress to return to their districts on a regular basis and thereby ease the stress both of relocating and of running for election every two years.

The Diversity of Members

The members serving in the modern House of Representatives more closely reflect the American population than at any other time in history. In 1916, Jeannette Rankin became the first woman to be elected to the House, and by the opening of the One-hundredth Congress in 1987, 104 women had served or were serving in the House. Many of the early women members were elected to finish out the terms of their deceased husbands, but over the past two decades the majority of women in Congress have been elected in their own right. Some women elected to fill their husband's seat have gone on to substantial careers of their own. Edith Nourse Rogers of Massachusetts was elected in 1925 to fill her husband's seat and served for 35 years. In 1977, the

In 1972, Barbara Jordan of Texas became the first southern black woman to win election to the House. Jordan served as a member of the House Judiciary Committee in the investigation of the Watergate break-in.

Congressional Women's Caucus was formed to give members of Congress an opportunity to meet and discuss issues concerning women and to decide on a course of legislative action.

In the mid-20th century, blacks began to reenter Congress for the first time since Reconstruction. Oscar DePriest was elected from Illinois in 1928 and a few other blacks from northern urban districts followed him during the next 30 years. But only in the 1960s and 1970s did blacks begin to regularly win election to the House. In 1972 Barbara Jordan of Texas and Andrew Young of Georgia became the first blacks from the South to win election since the 19th century. In 1971 a group of black congressmen organized the Congressional Black Caucus in order to provide a stronger voice for blacks in every congressional district.

The arrival of women and blacks in Congress has been only the most noticeable evidence of the diversity of the modern House. In the 1960s more Catholics and Jews won election to what had always been an overwhelmingly Protestant body. Hispanics began to win more seats in the 1970s and 1980s. The occupational makeup of the Congress, however, has not changed much in recent years. In the 1980s lawyers still constituted the largest group, and banking and business professionals were close behind. The average age of a representative in 1981 was 48—a decline of only 2 years over a period of 4 decades.

The Budget

The modern House is a far more expensive operation than the 19th-century Congresses, which often met for six or fewer months a year and required very little support staff. Today, the Congress convenes every January 3 and remains in session through most of the year. The House of Representatives, as the source of all spending bills, is responsible for establishing its own budget. In the annual legislative budget, the House and Senate appropriate from the public treasury the funds that they believe are necessary for the operation of Congress. These funds cover the members' own salaries, staff salaries, and the maintenance costs of the Capitol complex. By the 1980s, the annual budget for the House, the Senate, and the maintenance and operation of the Capitol building was more than $1.25 billion.

Voters wait patiently to enter voting booths during an off-year congressional election. Traditionally, fewer people vote in the years that fall between presidential elections.

The House Ways and Means Committee Hearing Room. Committees often hold hearings when members are considering bills of great controversy or importance.

FIVE

The Legislative Process

As freshmen members of the House of Representatives quickly learn, the job of translating ideas about policy into law requires a thorough knowledge of the legislative process. The House of Representatives has developed a complicated procedure for considering the 10,000 or more bills (proposed laws) that are introduced during the 2-year term of a Congress. This volume of bills, only six percent of which are enacted into law, reflects the variety of constituents represented by each member and the complicated affairs of modern government. This burden of legislation and the number of representatives have forced the House to develop a strictly regulated legislative process. Since the 18th century members have recognized that the size of the House created special problems that are not found in the Senate. Today, the House adheres to a legislative process that restricts individual members much more than in the Senate; a single senator has the power to halt action on any bill during its various stages of consideration.

The rules governing the legislative process in the House have always been the subject of controversy. The party in power naturally establishes rules and procedures favorable to its policy program. At times, the rules become the center of power struggles between senior and junior members or regional interests. The rules are also in a constant state of evolution. At the opening of every Congress the caucus of the majority party makes changes in the rules. But if the particulars of the legislative process are subject to debate, members of Congress have always understood that strict control over the consideration of bills is necessary in order to ensure that this complex body is capable of translating proposals into law. Today, the legislative process in the House of Representatives is at once more structured than ever and more open to the participation of a broad spectrum of members.

Only a member of the House of Representatives is qualified to submit a bill for consideration. Members with a proposal of their own might draft a bill with the help of the Office of the Legislative Counsel, a group of lawyers trained in the technical language of lawmaking and employed by the House to assist in drafting legislation. Often the member submits a bill for a special-interest group from his or her district. Still other bills are proposals a member has received from an individual constituent. Introduction of constituent legislation is part of the representative's duty and does not always reflect the representative's own views.

The most important source of legislative proposals in the modern House is the executive branch. The executive proposals may be part of the president's legislative program announced at the beginning of each session of Congress. Other bills from the executive branch include recommendations from experts in cabinet departments or agencies. The bills prepared by the executive branch are usually submitted by the chairman of the relevant committee or, if the president's party is the minority in the House, by the highest-ranking minority member of the committee. Whatever the source of legislation, the member submits the bill by handing it to the Clerk of the House or placing it in the "hopper," a box in use throughout the history of Congress.

Bills, which become law when approved by both houses of Congress and signed by the president, are the most common type of legislative proposal. The House also considers joint resolutions, which when approved by both houses and the president also have the force of law. The joint resolution is little different from a bill although it often applies to a single issue that needs immediate attention, such as emergency funding. Unless the resolution is submitted by the majority party's leadership, the bill goes through the entire legislative process. Concurrent resolutions, passed by both houses, and simple resolutions, passed by only one house, do not require presidential approval and are not laws, nor do they have the force of law. These resolutions generally express the opinion of the legislature on a current issue or concern adminis-trative matters in a single house, for example, amending rules of procedure.

President Gerald Ford presents his State of the Union message to the Ninety-fourth Congress in 1977. The president reveals his legislative agenda for the upcoming year in this annual speech.

Union Calendar No. 52

99TH CONGRESS
1ST SESSION

H. R. 2475

[Report No. 99–87]

To amend the Internal Revenue Code of 1954 to simplify the imputed interest rules of sections 1274 and 483, and for other purposes.

IN THE HOUSE OF REPRESENTATIVES

MAY 14, 1985

Mr. ROSTENKOWSKI (for himself, Mr. PICKLE, Mr. RANGEL, Mr. STARK, Mr. JONES of Oklahoma, Mr. JACOBS, Mr. FORD of Tennessee, Mr. JENKINS, Mr. HEFTEL of Hawaii, Mr. FOWLER, Mr. GUARINI, Mr. MATSUI, Mr. ANTHONY, Mr. FLIPPO, Mr. DORGAN of North Dakota, Mrs. KENNELLY, Mr. COYNE, Mr. DUNCAN, Mr. VANDER JAGT, Mr. FRENZEL, Mr. GRADISON, Mr. MOORE, Mr. THOMAS of California, Mr. DAUB, Mr. GREGG, and Mr. DASCHLE) introduced the following bill; which was referred to the Committee on Ways and Means

MAY 14, 1985

Committed to the Committee of the Whole House on the State of the Union and ordered to be printed

---

A BILL

To amend the Internal Revenue Code of 1954 to simplify the imputed interest rules of sections 1274 and 483, and for other purposes.

1 *Be it enacted by the Senate and House of Representa-*

2 *tives of the United States of America in Congress assembled,*

*　　*　　*　　*　　*　　*　　*

(Sample copy of first page and end of last page of this 16-page reported bill)

*　　*　　*　　*　　*　　*　　*

14 (4) TECHNICAL CORRECTION.—The amendment

15 made by paragraph (6) of section 3(b) shall apply as if

16 included in the amendments made by section 111 of

17 the Tax Reform Act of 1984.

After a House bill has been introduced by a sponsoring representative, it is assigned a number and referred to the proper committee for consideration.

Once a member submits a bill to the Clerk or places it in the hopper, the Speaker of the House, acting through the Parliamentarian, refers the proposal to a committee for consideration. The Parliamentarian determines by the wording of a bill which committee should receive it. Once a committee asserts its authority over a certain subject, the chairman and members jealously guard their jurisdiction.

The committee has almost complete authority over bills within its area. (For example, the Committee on the Judiciary has authority over such measures as those relating to judicial proceedings, Constitutional amendments, civil liberties, patents, and copyrights.) Through the committee process more than 80 percent of legislative proposals die without ever reaching a vote. The first step of the committee is usually to study the bill in a subcommittee. The members of the subcommittee specialize in some particular area under the full committee's jurisdiction and work with staff members to explore the potential effect of a bill. The subcommittee's study often includes hearings with witnesses who are knowledgeable about the bill's subject or who would be affected if the measure became law. In recent years these hearings have been held in public unless they concern matters of national security. The hearings of the subcommittee frequently result in amendments to the bill. The subcommittee then reports the bill to the full committee with its recommendation for approval or rejection.

The House Select Committee on Aging, chaired by Representative Claude Pepper of Florida (second from right). The committee holds hearings on problems of the elderly and oversees all federal programs that affect the elderly, such as Medicare and Social Security.

On matters of great importance or controversy the full committee might hold its own hearings. On more common bills the committee proceeds to a vote on the prepared bill, with or without amendments. If a majority of the committee or just the chairman disapproves of the bill, the chairman usually rejects it by refusing to take any action. The committee can also completely rewrite a bill or vote to reject it. If the committee approves the bill, it also prepares a report to accompany the legislation when it comes before the full House for debate and a vote. These reports not only help members decide how to vote, but also aid the courts in interpreting the act after it goes into effect.

As a first step in the floor action on a bill, each bill reported out of committee (that is, returned after consideration) is placed on one of five calendars according to either the established rules of the House or the requests of members. The Union Calendar, House Calendar, Consent Calendar, Private Calendar, and Discharge Calendar, which are distinguished by the subject matter of the bills, determine when and how the House will consider a measure. Under House rules, the Union Calendar includes all bills regarding the appropriation of public funds. (The majority of public bills and resolutions are placed on the Union Calendar.) House rules stipulate that public bills which do not have any connection with appropriations are placed on the House Calendar and considered by the full House. Members may request that bills on a noncontroversial subject be considered on the Consent Calendar in order to vote on them quickly and without debate. Twice a month, the House's rules provide for consideration of a Private Calendar filled with bills that affect individuals—for instance, bills for relief in matters concerning immigration and naturalization. The least-used schedule, the Discharge Calendar, is intended for bills that a majority of members insist on reporting to the floor despite the opposition of the committee authorized to consider the measure. Petitions for discharge are seldom used and even less seldom successful.

Before a bill comes up on the appropriate calendar, the Rules Committee establishes the guidelines by which the House will consider the legislation. This enormously powerful committee determines the time limit for debate and the opportunities for amending each bill. Since the Rules Committee was established in 1880, it has worked in close accord with the House leadership, and its rules are generally approved by the whole House. One exception was the tenure of Rules Committee chairman Howard Smith of Virginia, who used his position to prevent consideration of civil rights legislation supported by the House leadership in the 1960s. This kind of obstruction became less likely after 1974, when the Democratic Caucus gave the Speaker of the House authority to select the majority members of the Rules Committee and thereby secure support for his legislative program.

The first step in the House's full consideration of a bill is the vote on the rules developed by the Rules Committee. Most major bills, and all bills on the Union Calendar, are then considered in the Committee of the Whole House on the State of the Union, usually referred to as the Committee of the Whole. This is a device developed by the English Parliament to allow free debate without the presence of the Speaker, who in Britain was allied with the Crown and might report to the monarch on the substance of the debate. In modern times the procedure is used to allow a smaller quorum (a minimum of 100 members rather than the 218 required in the full House) and permit a shorter time for debate on amendments. As in the historical committee in Britain, the current Committee of the Whole has more flexible rules than the full House and allows a broader participation in debate. When the full House resolves into the Committee of the Whole, it carries out two rituals that date back to the English Parliament. The mace—a rod that symbolizes the authority of the Speaker— is moved by the sergeant at arms to a position below the podium to signify the Speaker's lack of authority over the Committee of the Whole. Then the Speaker leaves the podium and appoints a member of his party to serve as chairman of the Committee of the Whole.

During the debate on a bill the chairman and the ranking minority member of the committee that reported the bill act as floor managers. The time allotted for debate is evenly divided between the two floor managers, one from the majority and one from the minority party. Even if the minority member supports the committee chairman, his or her time is given to opponents of the bill. The floor managers begin the debate on a bill and then yield the time that remains to others in their party. After the floor managers present their position, the House, still in the Committee of the Whole, considers amendments. It is the job of the majority party's floor manager to get the bill through with as few amendments as possible.

After votes on amendments have been taken, the Committee of the Whole reports the bill, with any changes, to the full House, and the Speaker returns to his chair on the podium in order to preside over the full House. Some member usually makes a motion to order the "previous question." This is a device to cut off debate and take final action on the bill. First the members vote whether to include in the bill any amendments approved in the Committee of the Whole. After this vote, opponents of the bill have a final chance to stop the measure. A motion to recommit the bill to committee, if adopted, ends House consideration of that bill without a final vote. Committees seldom reconsider any bills recommitted to them. A motion to recommit with instructions attempts to send the bill back for amendment and has only slightly more chance of being considered. Neither of these motions succeed very often. The final

This silver mace was made for the House of Representatives in 1841. The House has traditionally used the mace to open the Committee of the Whole House, which represents the full House but needs only 100 members to form a quorum.

A conference committee resolves differences over a bill. Such committees, made up of members of both houses of Congress, meet in secret and must make a compromise between the two houses' versions of the bill before it can become law.

vote is then taken and, if approved by a majority of members present, the bill is sent on for consideration by the Senate.

When the House or Senate receives a bill passed by the other body, they each refer the measure to committee for consideration, much the same way as they do for original legislation. By the time a bill is passed through the legislative process in the other house, it almost always is amended or revised in some fashion. The differences between a House and Senate version of a bill must be worked out in a conference committee called by the body that originated the legislation. The Speaker of the House, in consultation with the chairman of the committee that reported the bill, selects the House members who will serve on the conference committee. The House and Senate conferees have authority to discuss only those provisions of a bill that differ in the two versions. But in practice, the conference committee often alters parts of the bill that read the same in each house. These changes in the uncontested portions of a bill are usually part of the bargaining process by which the representatives and senators iron out an agreement.

When a conference committee reaches a final accord on a bill, it prepares a report, which includes a revised version of the bill that is then submitted to the full House under regulations set by the Rules Committee. A conference report has high priority in legislative business and may interrupt consideration of another bill. If the House votes to accept the report, the bill has passed in that chamber. If the Senate also approves the report, the bill is sent first to the Speaker of the House for his signature and then to the president of the Senate, who is the vice-president of the United States. The president then receives the bill and has 10 days within which to sign it into law. If the president opposes the legislation he may return the bill with a message explaining his veto. The bill may then become law only if two-thirds of both houses of Congress vote to override the president's veto. The legislature may override a presidential veto at any time in a given Congress. Sometimes when the president opposes a bill but does not want to risk the loss of prestige involved in an override vote in Congress, he simply does not return the bill, thereby allowing it to become law with his "pocket approval." A bill becomes law 10 days after passage by both houses only if Congress remains in session. If Congress adjourns within 10 days of passing a bill, the president can "pocket veto" the measure by simply not returning it.

Since 1974 the House has observed an additional step in the legislative process to approve the annual budget for the federal government. According to the Congressional Budget and Impoundment Control Act of 1974, the president submits his proposed annual budget on January 20 of each year. Congress attempted to prevent presidential impoundments—forbidding an executive branch agency to spend money even though the funding had been appropriated by Congress—and to become less dependent on the president's budget proposals. The House and Senate each created a Committee on the Budget to consider the executive branch's requests and draw up their own recommendations. In April of each year the committees report to their respective bodies a resolution establishing targets for spending and revenue levels for the fiscal year beginning the following October 1. The Congress must agree to a first budget resolution before May 15. Only then may the House of Representatives begin to consider bills reported by the Committee on Appropriations or changes in the revenue laws. In September, after approval of all regular appropriation bills, Congress passes a second budget resolution in which its initial targets can be revised and can force a reconsideration of appropriation bills that exceeded the limits set in May.

This complicated budget process was intended to give the Congress greater control over the president's annual budget requests. The president could propose to rescind, or cancel, enacted appropriations, but only if Congress agreed (with a majority vote in both the House and the Senate) to the rescission within 45 days. Otherwise, the money appropriated must be spent

House Speaker Jim Wright signs the final version of a bill. After a bill is approved by both houses of Congress, it is sent to the president of the United States for his signature.

93

Three members of the 1981 House Budget Committee confer. This committee reviews the annual federal budget and appropriation proposals for government agencies and public institutions.

by the executive branch. In recent years, however, Congress has not always been able to meet the deadlines established by the act and has passed continuing resolutions that allow the government to operate on temporary funds until a regular appropriation has been passed. The Balanced Budget and Emergency Deficit Reduction Act of 1985 (known by the names of its sponsors, Gramm, Rudman, and Hollings) revised the original budget act in order to set specific limits on the annual deficit (shortage of funds). This act temporarily eliminated the second budget resolution and made the first resolution binding on the House and Senate.

The Gramm-Rudman-Hollings Act set maximum allowable deficit levels on a declining basis from 1986 to 1991, when the budget must be balanced—that is, the deficit must be at zero. The bill required the president to bring future federal budgets into line with the deficit-reduction schedule by reducing or eliminating cost-of-living allowances and other automatic spending increases previously enacted in other benefits programs. But by allowing the president to suspend such increases, Congress would be granting the president sole authority to limit or refuse whatever legal rights the recipients had to the increased payments. The first version of the bill gave the comptroller general of the General Accounting Office (an independent agency that controls and audits the federal government's expenditures and acts as an agent of the

94

Congress) the final word in ordering the president to pare spending and reduce deficits.

However, on July 7, 1986, the U.S. Supreme Court declared the automatic provisions of the budget-balancing law unconstitutional. The court ruled that the law's mechanism for spending cuts violated the principle of the separation of powers because it granted the executive branch authority to a legislative branch officer, the comptroller general (who could be removed from office by a vote of Congress).

Whatever the problems of the budget-balancing measure have been in the past, it has forced Congress and the president to make difficult choices about domestic spending, military spending, and taxes. The budget process, perhaps the most important business of the House of Representatives, remains subject to considerable controversy and is likely to change in the near future.

In a House committee room, hearings are filmed by a television crew. Since 1979 telecasts have given the American public a closer view of their representatives' work.

SIX

Prospect for the Future

Since the inauguration of the federal government in 1789, the greatest challenge before the House of Representatives has been the task of giving voice to its numerous and diverse constituencies while managing an effective and productive legislative assembly. Designed to meet contemporary demands on this branch of Congress, the reforms of legislative organization and the budget process during the 1970s were the latest in a long series of changes in the internal structure of the House. The challenge before the House of Representatives perhaps has never been so great or the threat to effective legislation so serious as today, when 435 members must each represent diverse populations seeking particular policies and programs from the federal government.

Certainly the House of Representatives will find it necessary to continue internal reorganization in order to deal with the ever-increasing load of legislation it faces in each new Congress. Particularly in the specialized work of committees and subcommittees, representatives must handle a formidable amount of technical legislation. The expanded scope of the federal government since the New Deal and World War II has placed a burden on the appropriations process in the House and increased Congress's responsibility for overseeing expenditures carried out by the executive branch.

In addition to the legislative demands on the House of Representatives, members of this branch of Congress face the need to finance campaigns every two years. In an age when even local elections depend largely on television coverage, campaign financing becomes more and more important for members seeking reelection. As the population grows and the number of representatives remains constant, each member's campaign must reach a larger number of constituents. Candidates for the House of Representatives must either be wealthy themselves or raise vast amounts of money from supporters.

Since 1979, when the House began regular telecasts of its daily sessions, the legislative process has been exposed to public scrutiny as never before. This exposure gives a broad audience a chance to understand the business of Congress, but at the same time it places pressure on the House to operate as an efficient and responsive legislature.

Perhaps the most serious problem facing the House and the Congress as a whole is the expanded power of the presidency during the past half century. Created as a coequal branch of government, the presidency has in recent years taken the lead in initiating legislative policy. The president's dominance has been most evident in the conduct of foreign affairs through the appropriation of funds that allows a president to carry out his defense and foreign policy proposals. In the years since World War II, when the president has controlled an enormous defense and intelligence establishment, Congress has had difficulty overseeing the execution of a foreign policy that presidents claim requires secrecy and the ability to respond quickly without consultation with congressional leaders. The exact distribution of authority between the Congress and the presidency remains an unsettled issue.

The House of Representatives has continuously evolved to meet new demands on the federal government, as old responses have often become insufficient. Since the days of Speaker Henry Clay, political parties have provided the most effective means of organizing the House. In recent years, however, congressional leaders have noted a decline in party loyalty. Many members are more responsive to constituent demands and interest groups in their districts than to the legislative policy of their party's leaders. Parties will probably remain a central means of organizing the House, but party leaders may have to recognize and accommodate these local interests in formulating their legislative policy.

The Constitution created the House of Representatives to develop in unison with the growth of the nation. Today, the House, despite its increased size and the demands of complex legislation, continues to carry out the basic mandate of the Constitution. Through reapportionment and elections every two years,

Georgia congressman Elliott Levitas talks to a constituent about current issues. Representatives maintain contact with voters by frequently visiting their home districts and communicating through the local media.

the House remains the branch of government most closely representative of the views of the population. Even after the tremendous expansion in the size and role of the government, the House has maintained its prerogatives over tax legislation and the appropriations process. The regular reexamination and revision of House procedure will enable this legislature to evolve to meet the duties outlined in the Constitution.

House of Representatives

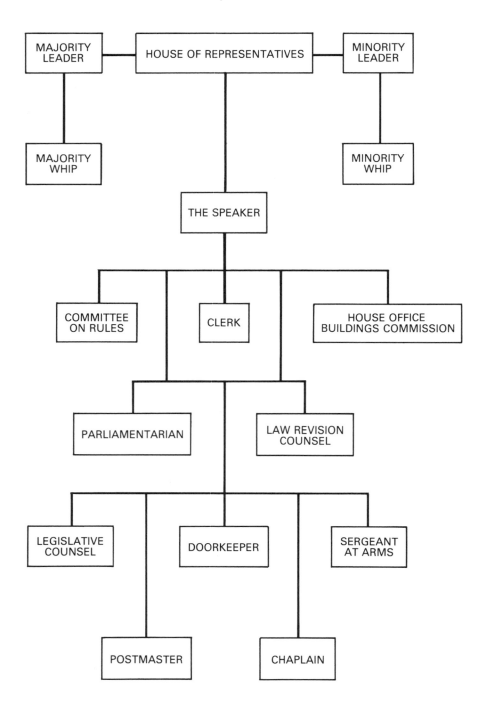

GLOSSARY

Apportionment The allocation of legislative seats; in the U.S. House of Representatives, legislative seats are allocated based on state populations.

Calendar An agenda that contains the names of bills or resolutions to be considered before committees or in either the House or Senate.

Caucus A closed meeting of party members for the purpose of selecting party leaders and deciding on legislative positions.

Checks and balances Constitutional grant of powers that ensures each of the three branches of government a sufficient role in the actions of the others, so that no one branch may dominate the others.

Constituent A resident of a legislative district.

Concurrent resolution A special measure passed by one house of Congress with the other concurring, but not requiring the president's signature; used to make or amend joint rules or to express the sentiment of Congress.

Impeachment A formal accusation, rendered by the House, that commits an accused civil official to trial by the Senate.

Implied powers Powers given to Congress to do whatever is necessary and proper to carry out the powers delegated to it in the Constitution.

Joint committee A legislative committee composed of members of both the House and the Senate, usually intended to study an issue of common interest or speed up legislative action.

Joint resolution A measure, similar to a bill, that must be approved in both houses and by the president.

Override An action by Congress to try to reverse a presidential veto of legislation by means of an affirmative vote of two-thirds in both houses.

Platform A statement of principles and objectives promoted by a party or candidate that is used during a campaign to win support from voters.

101

Pocket veto   A special veto power exercised at the end of a legislative session whereby bills not signed by the president die after a specified time period. If the president holds a bill for 10 days without signing it and Congress adjourns during the 10 days, then the bill is pocket vetoed.

Quorum   The minimum number of members of a legislative chamber who must be present in order to transact business. In the House, 218 members constitute a quorum.

Rules Committee   A standing committee that provides special rules under which specific bills will be debated, amended, and considered by the House.

Select committee   A committee established for a limited time period and for a special purpose, such as the Select Committee on Hunger.

Separation of powers   Constitutional division of power among legislative, executive, and judicial branches.

Standing committee   A committee of a legislative body that considers bills within a subject area; for example, the Committee on Agriculture or the Committee on the Judiciary.

SELECTED REFERENCES

Bolling, Richard. *Power in the House: A History of the Leadership of the House of Representatives.* New York: Putnam, 1968.

Bowen, Catherine Drinker. *Miracle at Philadelphia.* Boston: Little, Brown, 1966.

Burns, James M., J. W. Peltason, and Thomas E. Cronin. *Government By the People.* Thirteenth Edition. Englewood Cliffs, NJ: Prentice-Hall, 1987.

Cheney, Richard B., and Lynne V. Cheney. *Kings of the Hill: Power and Personality in the House of Representatives.* New York: Crossroad, 1983.

Congressional Quarterly. *Guide to Congress.* Third Edition. Washington, DC: Congressional Quarterly, 1983.

Josephy, Alvin M., Jr. *On the Hill: A History of the American Congress.* New York: Simon & Schuster, 1979.

MacNeil, Neil. *Forge of Democracy: The House of Representatives.* New York: David McKay, 1963.

Madison, James. *Notes of Debates in the Federal Convention of 1787 Reported by James Madison.* Introduction by Adrienne Koch. Athens, OH: Ohio University Press, 1985.

Mikva, Abner, Jr., and Patti B. Sarris. *The American Congress: The First Branch.* New York: Franklin Watts, 1983.

Neal, Harry E. *Diary of Democracy. The Story of Political Parties in America.* New York: Julian Messner, 1963.

Oleszek, Walter J. *Congressional Procedure and the Policy Process.* Second Edition. Washington, DC: Congressional Quarterly, 1984.

O'Neill, Thomas P., Jr. *Man of the House: The Life and Political Memoirs of Speaker Tip O'Neill.* New York: Random House, 1987.

Willett, Edward F., Jr., ed. *How Our Laws Are Made.* Washington, DC: U.S. Government Printing Office, 1986.

INDEX

Bruce A. Ragsdale is associate historian in the Office for the Bicentennial in the United States House of Representatives. He is coeditor of the *Biographical Directory of the United States Congress* (1988) and was a researcher for the Papers of George Washington project from 1979 to 1985. He holds a Ph.D. in American history from the University of Virginia and has taught history there and at the Catholic University of America in Washington, D.C.

Arthur M. Schlesinger, jr., served in the White House as special assistant to Presidents Kennedy and Johnson. He is the author of numerous acclaimed works in American history at Harvard College and has twice been awarded the Pulitzer Prize. He taught history at Harvard College for many years and is currently Albert Schweitzer Professor of the Humanities at the City College of New York.

PICTURE CREDITS